COMPLEX EMERGENCIES:
Bureaucratic Arrangements
in the
U.N. Secretariat

COMPLEX EMERGENCIES:

Bureaucratic Arrangements in the U.N. Secretariat

EDWARD MARKS

National Defense University Press
Washington, DC
1996

National Defense University Press Publications

To increase general knowledge and inform discussion, the Institute for National Strategic Studies, through its publication arm the NDU Press, publishes *Strategic Forums*; McNair Papers; proceedings of University- and Institute-sponsored symposia; books relating to U.S. national security, especially to issues of joint, combined, or coalition warfare, peacekeeping operations, and national strategy; and a variety of other works designed to circulate contemporary comment and offer alternatives to current policy. The Press occasionally publishes out-of-print defense classics, historical works, and other especially timely or distinguished writing on national security.

For more information about NDU Press publications, please call 202/685-4210, or write to NDU Press/INSS, Bldg. 62, 300 5th Avenue, Ft. McNair, Washington, DC 20319, or visit our home page at http://www.ndu.edu/cgi-bin/wais.pl.

Library of Congress Cataloging-in-Publication Data

Marks, Edward, 1934-
     Complex emergencies: bureaucratic arrangements in the U.N. Secretariat / Edward Marks.
        p.   cm.
     1. United Nations. Secretariat. 2. United Nations—Armed Forces. 3. United Nations Emergency Force. I. Title.
     JX1977.A362M37 1996
     354. 1'03—dc20   96-8373
                                                         CIP

First Printing, October 1996

CONTENTS

Foreword

The end of the Cold War opened a Pandora's box of local conflicts around the world. These crises often call for peacekeeping or humanitarian assistance operations, and sometimes for a combination of the two. For a multitude of reasons, these operations have moved up the priority list of potential missions for the American military and other U.S. Government agencies. Recent deployments to locales as far apart as Rwanda and Haiti and missions as disparate as famine relief in Somalia and maintaining peacekeeping forces in Bosnia are obvious examples.

U.S. involvement in peacekeeping and humanitarian assistance is often pursued in a multinational framework, usually involving the United Nations. At the urging of the United States and other nations, the U.N. Headquarters in New York has been reorganized in recent years to improve its management of these types of complex emergencies. Three new U.N. Secretariat organizations have been created: the Departments of Political Affairs, Peacekeeping Operations, and Humanitarian Affairs. Even though the United States was a major player in the reform movement that produced these new entities, American officials still have little experience with or knowledge of these departments, which are still very much in the early "shake down" stages of development.

To help U.S. Government operators function effectively with the new U.N. departments, the author—Edward Marks, a U.S. Ambassador with extensive experience in this area—has produced this guide. Ambassador Marks describes in detail the capabilities and functions of the new bureaucracies, appending useful information on the missions, budget, and structure of each. This handbook should help orient the increasing numbers of U.S. operators, military and civilian alike, who may well find themselves working with the United Nations on a peacekeeping or humanitarian mission.

ERVIN J. ROKKE
Lieutenant General, U.S. Air Force
President, National Defense University

COMPLEX EMERGENCIES:
Bureaucratic Arrangements in the U.N. Secretariat

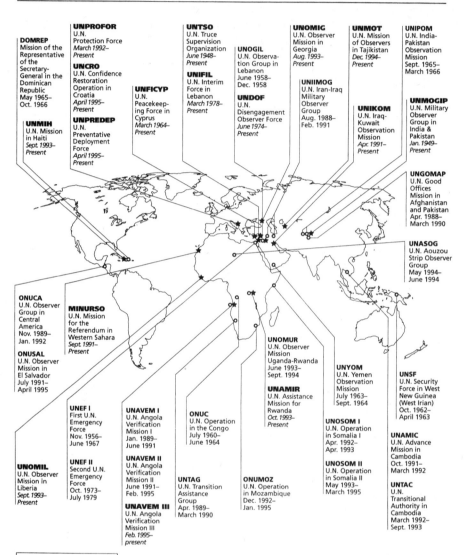

DOMREP
U.N.
Mission of the
Representative
of the
Secretary-
General in the
Dominican
Republic
May 1965–
Oct. 1966

UNMIH
U.N. Mission
in Haiti
Sept. 1993–
Present

UNPROFOR
U.N.
Protection Force
March 1992–
Present

UNCRO
U.N. Confidence
Restoration
Operation in
Croatia
April 1995–
Present

UNPREDEP
U.N.
Preventative
Deployment
Force
April 1995–
Present

UNFICYP
U.N.
Peacekeep-
ing Force in
Cyprus
March 1964–
Present

UNTSO
U.N. Truce
Supervision
Organization
June 1948–
Present

UNIFIL
U.N. Interim
Force in
Lebanon
March 1978–
Present

UNOGIL
U.N. Observa-
tion Group in
Lebanon
June 1958–
Dec. 1958

UNDOF
U.N.
Disengagement
Observer Force
June 1974–
Present

UNOMIG
U.N. Observer
Mission in
Georgia
Aug. 1993–
Present

UNIIMOG
U.N. Iran-Iraq
Military
Observer
Group
Aug. 1988–
Feb. 1991

UNMOT
U.N. Mission
of Observers
in Tajikistan
Dec. 1994–
Present

UNIKOM
U.N. Iraq-
Kuwait
Observation
Mission
Apr. 1991–
Present

UNIPOM
U.N. India-
Pakistan
Observation
Mission
Sept. 1965–
March 1966

UNMOGIP
U.N. Military
Observer
Group in
India &
Pakistan
Jan. 1949–
Present

UNGOMAP
U.N. Good
Offices
Mission in
Afghanistan
and Pakistan
Apr. 1988–
March 1990

UNASOG
U.N. Aouzou
Strip Observer
Group
May 1994–
June 1994

ONUCA
U.N. Observer
Group in
Central
America
Nov. 1989–
Jan. 1992

ONUSAL
U.N. Observer
Mission in
El Salvador
July 1991–
April 1995

MINURSO
U.N. Mission
for the
Referendum in
Western Sahara
Sept. 1991–
Present

UNOMUR
U.N. Observer
Mission
Uganda-Rwanda
June 1993–
Sept. 1994

UNAMIR
U.N. Assistance
Mission for
Rwanda
Oct. 1993–
Present

UNYOM
U.N. Yemen
Observation
Mission
July 1963–
Sept. 1964

UNSF
U.N. Security
Force in West
New Guinea
(West Irian)
Oct. 1962–
April 1963

UNEF I
First U.N.
Emergency
Force
Nov. 1956–
June 1967

UNEF II
Second U.N.
Emergency
Force
Oct. 1973–
July 1979

UNOMIL
U.N. Observer
Mission in
Liberia
Sept. 1993–
Present

UNAVEM I
U.N. Angola
Verification
Mission I
Jan. 1989–
June 1991

UNAVEM II
U.N. Angola
Verification
Mission II
June 1991–
Feb. 1995

UNAVEM III
U.N. Angola
Verification
Mission III
Feb. 1995–
present

ONUC
U.N. Operation
in the Congo
July 1960–
June 1964

UNTAG
U.N. Transition
Assistance
Group
Apr. 1989–
March 1990

ONUMOZ
U.N. Operation
in Mozambique
Dec. 1992–
Jan. 1995

UNOSOM I
U.N. Operation
in Somalia I
Apr. 1992–
Apr. 1993

UNOSOM II
U.N. Operation
in Somalia II
May 1993–
March 1995

UNAMIC
U.N. Advance
Mission in
Cambodia
Oct. 1991–
March 1992

UNTAC
U.N.
Transitional
Authority in
Cambodia
March 1992–
Sept. 1993

○ **Completed Missions: 22**
★ **Ongoing Missions: 16**

TOTAL MISSIONS: 38

Based on U.N. information.
Compiled by the PROJECT ON PEACEKEEPING & THE UNITED NATIONS
Council for a Livable World Education Fund
110 Maryland Ave. NE, Washington, DC 20002 (202)543-4100

Peacekeeping: A History

Organizing the Department of Humanitarian Assistance while trying to
deal with ongoing emergencies is like trying to install spark plugs in your
car's motor while participating in a Formula I race.

Ambassador Jan Eliasson
First Under-Secretary-General for Humanitarian Affairs

Prior to the end of the Cold War, the interest of the United States in
U.N. peacekeeping operations was marginal, both with respect to
policy and to operations. The Cold War rivalry between the United States
and the USSR ensured that the United Nations would undertake
peacekeeping operations only when permitted by both super powers and
therefore, almost by definition, in situations of limited scope and import.

As a consequence, and despite U.N. Secretary-General
Hammarskjold's effort in the late 1950s and the early 1960s to create a
more robust U.N. role in what he called "Chapter 6 1/2 operations," the
U.N. organizational and managerial capacity for conducting
peacekeeping operations remained minimal: a handful of officials
attached to the Secretary-General and a skeletal logistical organization.
These organizational arrangements proved adequate for the type of
peacekeeping operations mounted in the Cold War era.

The United States participated only in a limited manner in so-called
traditional peacekeeping operations, except in the Security Council
decisionmaking. The Military Staff Committee, called for in the U.N.
Charter, had never blossomed as a significant U.N. institution. No other
serious military relations developed, although a small number of
individual U.S. military officers and technicians were from time to time
assigned to specific peacekeeping operations, as in Lebanon and the
Golan Heights. Accordingly, U.S. policy makers and operations,
especially in the security area, had little to do with this part of the United
Nations and correspondingly little interest in it.

The dramatic expansion of U.N. peacekeeping and the introduction
of large-scale U.N. led humanitarian assistance operations in the past 5
years, however, have changed this situation and created a much more
extensive relationship between the United States, and especially its
Armed Forces, and the United Nations. In Somalia and now in the
territories of the successor states to the Socialist Republic of Yugoslavia,
U.S. military and civilian personnel have played and are playing major
roles, with thousands of American servicemen and women and civilian
personnel being deployed. Even when the United States is the principal

manager of a specific operation, the desirability and necessity of working with forces and personnel from other countries and with U.N. officials require close working relations with the United Nations.

It is in this context that recent organizational changes and developments in the United Nations headquarters in New York are of relevance to U.S. Government planners and operators, especially those in the Department of Defense. Various governments, led by the United States, began to urge organizational reform in New York as early as 1989, with particular emphasis on humanitarian assistance and the management of peacekeeping operations. The minimal organization arrangements existed in the U.N. headquarters for peacekeeping purposes were clearly no longer adequate as the scale of peacekeeping operations expanded. Many governments, and again especially the United States, backed up their recommendations with offers of assistance in the form of additional funds, personnel, and technical assistance. These efforts have produced a rationalization and an expansion of the U.N. peacekeeping and humanitarian assistance bureaucracy, notably the creation of three new headquarters departments: Political Affairs, Peacekeeping Operations, and Humanitarian Affairs.

The purpose of this publication is to provide a photograph of these organizational developments as of mid-1995. The three departments are now up and running and have become the essential partner of the United States in the whole range of peacekeeping and humanitarian assistance operations. However, their role and their capabilities are still in flux and their future depends upon the degree to which they actually contribute to the success of specific operations. The United States has a vested interest in these departments, given our role in creating them, and a policy interest in their success, given the likelihood of their being our partners in some multilateral operations.

This paper, therefore, is a primer, a guide to the key decision makers and operators in U.N. Headquarters for American officials responsible for U.S. participation in multilateral peacekeeping and humanitarian assistance operations.

I. The Problem and the Response

Background

In its first 43 years the Security Council authorized and the United Nations implemented 13 peacekeeping operations. In the 43 *months* from 1988 to 1992, U.N. Member States authorized 13 additional operations, and the number of U.N. peacekeeping forces (military and civilian) deployed around the world jumped from about 11,500 in late 1991 to approximately 80,000 by the end of 1993. Not only were these operations more numerous, but some, like Cambodia and the former Yugoslavia, were much bigger and more complicated than anything attempted previously and are generally refered to as "complex political emergencies." In addition to their fundamental political and military character, these operations commonly now contain a significant humananitarian component as large populations come under risk.

At the same time, serious humanitarian crises are erupting, arising from natural or human causes, some of which, as in Somalia, create the need for a peacekeeping operation. In both cases—complex political crises and complex humanitarian crises—the operations are increasingly multidimensional and require increasingly sophisticated headquarters directions and backup.

Even with the dramatic increase in both scope and scale in field operations in the late 1980s and early 1990s, the United Nations was able to find field personnel (military and civilian) more or less rapidly depending on the complexity and danger of the operation. But the headquarters mechanism for planning, supporting, and managing them was rapidly overcome. In 1991, the headquarters personnel available to perform these tasks amounted to about 100 staff officers, of whom only three were professional military.

Reorganization and enhancement of the Secretariat in New York was obviously necessary. The General Assembly started the process by debating and then creating a new department, the Department of Humanitarian Affairs. Growing pressure by various governments to convince the new Secretary-General to reorganize the unwieldy and top-heavy U.N. structure culminated in a pointed request by the Chief of State Summit session of the Security Council in February 1992, and was followed by extensive reorganization proposals by the Secretary-General.

By early 1995 a whole new organizational structure, admittedly still skeletal but nonetheless sound, for the management of complex emergencies was in place in New York. Three new departments (Political Affairs, Peacekeeping Operations, and Humanitarian Affairs) had been created and staffed and were well into actual management of field operations.

The information contained herein was obtained directly from U.N. officials in the three departments discussed, published or internal documents of the United Nations, U.S. Government officials in the Departments of State and Defense, and a few academic experts. None of this information is sensitive or controlled in any manner, but was made freely available in a spirit of openness and cooperation in the hope that greater transparency in the operations of the United Nations can only contribute to its effectiveness.

Management of U.N. Peacekeeping Up To the Late 1980s

U.N. Headquarters structure for managing peacekeeping operations was initiated by Secretary-General Dag Hammarskjold during the Suez Canal crisis in the mid-1950s. By the 1980s, responsibility for managing peacekeeping operations was located in the Office of Special Political Affairs and was handled by one of the two Under-Secretaries-General (USG) for Special Political Affairs. The other USG served as a mediator and troubleshooter for the Secretary-General. In 1988, the troubleshooter USG left the U.N. and that position abolished. The peacemaking functions of conflict mediation and political negotiation were moved into the Secretary-General's Executive Office where they were managed by the remaining political USG and separated from the operational side of peacekeeping.

The operational side, in turn, was divided into three parts. The Office of Special Political Affairs, with a staff of under three dozen, provided the headquarters management and liaison for the field missions. The Secretary-General's Military Advisor (a post created during the Congo crisis of 1960) and his small staff of four or five officers functioned as the military operations staff of peacekeeping operations. The Field Operations Division (FOD) in the Department of Administration and Management (approximately 60-70 officials) generated requirements for transport, logistical support and communications, drew up mission budgets, and tended to these aspects of each operation when deployed.

This low-key structure and decentralized structure functioned well in the comparatively low-key environment of U.N. peacekeeping in the Cold War period, at least according to the Rand Corporation: "It is mainly to the credit of a few outstanding individuals that the U.N. has become highly skilled at traditional peacekeeping, given the extremely cumbersome bureaucratic arrangements it employs" (Rand Corporation, Project Memorandum, "A Comparison of Five U.N. Peace Operations", March 1995). For a base of reference it should be noted that the *total* U.N. central Secretariat staff in 1990 was just under 14,000, of whom approximately 100 were directly involved in peacekeeping operations. Readers can compare these figures with those of their respective foreign affairs and defense ministries.

Humanitarian Affairs

On the humanitarian side, the United Nations has been dealing with emergencies for decades but these humanitarian crises (many of them natural disasters) were quite different from peacekeeping operations. The political/military and humanitarian relief elements of the United Nations were, before 1992, separate in terms of organization, finance, bureaucratic culture, location, and field operations.

Most observers are surprised to learn that approximately 75 percent of U.N. funds and personnel are involved in the system's economic and social areas—and that is true even today with the dramatic increase in peacekeeping operations. The vast bulk of this activity takes places in the UN's operational units and agencies such as UNICEF, the U.N. High Commissioner for Refugees, the World Food Program, the World Health Organization, and the U.N. Development Program. These are semi-autonomous institutions, each with its own mandate, intergovernmental governing council, field establishment, and, most important of all, independently raised budget. Their headquarters are dispersed geographicly, with only two in New York (UNDP and UNICEF), while the rest are in Geneva, Rome and a few other locales.

Each has been permanently deployed around the world, preoccupied with economic and social development, but also in varying degrees, with responding to refugee flows, famines, epidemics, and similar humanitarian crises. Some problems, such as those involving refugees, were handled by one specific agency, such as the U.N. High Commissioner for Refugees or the U.N. Disaster Relief Organization. Others required coordination among several of the so-called humanitarian agencies; such coordination generally taking place among field representatives under the very light hand of the U.N. Resident Representative in the country in question.

Over the years, these organizations have created their own particular bureaucratic cultures composed of a mix of general U.N. attitudes, their own mandates, and their own field experience (e.g. UNICEF concentrates on children and has a carefully cultivated public image directly related to its fundraising). These organizations do not take easily to centralized direction or coordination.

As a group they also have another concern, that of mixing humanitarian with political/military considerations. It is generally agreed among humanitarian aid workers that the principals of impartiality and neutrality are fundamental to humanitarian aid. Adherence to these principals can become difficult if U.N. humanitarian aid becomes linked to military and political interests of a Security Council mandate, as in Somalia, Cambodia, and northern Iraq. Thus, many advocate the need for "humanitarian space," that is, keeping some separate identity and functioning from U.N. military and political components.

The Department of Humanitarian Affairs (DHA) was created to deal with these problems,but continues to face the inevitable bureaucratic obstacles. Its mandate to coordinate among U.N. agencies runs against the tradition of operational autonomy, a desire to integrate the humanitarian agencies into more inclusive political-military-humanitarian operations, and the need to preserve a "humanitarian space" in complex emergencies.

Strains on the System

There was no particular need for interaction between these two sides of house until the late 1980s or early 1990s. However the immediate post-Cold War period saw a dramatic increase in crises of a character that mingled the two concerns—political/military and humanitarian—in what is characterized in the U.N. environment as "complex emergencies." These are crises of sufficient magnitude to engage the attention of the world community but of a restricted local character arising out of some combination of humanitarian crisis, breakdown of national political authority, or regional political confrontation that has moved into the violent stage. One important characteristic of this outbreak of crises is the tendency for them to be internal wars, such as in Somalia, Sudan, Cambodia, Angola, Rwanda, the former Yugoslavia, and Iraq. All pose a serious threat to the well-being of significant numbers of innocent people, and all make some claim on the attention of the international community for humanitarian and geopolitical reasons.

Like a teenager, U.N. peacekeeping has been both growing taller and gaining weight. With removal of the discipline of the bipolar relationship between two Super Powers, the international community is seeking methods for dealing with the Somalias and Bosnias of the post-Cold War world. The concern that such outbreaks of instability, combining both the phenomena of failing national societies and heartrending humanitarian crises, are "unpredictably explosive" and can seriously threaten international peace and security has produced an interest in a form of U.N. peacekeeping that far transcends the traditional deployment of a relatively small number of lightly armed "Blue Berets."

Traditional U.N. peacekeeping was, and is, a surgical instrument for specific and limited situations. The Pearson-Hammarskjold model of interpositional peacekeeping deployment dominated the international scene from 1956 until the early 1990s. It was invented in the Cold War era and, being consciously designed to deal with the realities of the Cold War, proved both useful and successful—but the post-Cold War world calls for more complicated surgery. This is the so-called Second Generation peacekeeping, a multidimensional activity combining traditional peacekeeping with extensive civilian responsibilities for humanitarian, human rights, electoral, and rehabilitation assistance. As former U.N. Under-Secretary for Humanitarian Affairs Jan Eliasson said, "If we have learned anything—not least from Somalia and the former Yugoslavia, but in dozens of humanitarian emergencies—it is that the U.N. should seek to integrate efforts at peacekeeping, peace making and humanitarian action as a part of peace building, and undertake them simultaneously to the maximum extent." In other words, peacekeeping in the post-Cold War world is a very different creature from the traditional activity authorized by the Security Council in response to specific if limited threats to international peace and security as called for in the U.N. Charter.

The cognoscenti know that the United Nations is not a government or even a decently integrated bureaucratic organization, especially in the political/military area. It is an association of Member States who have ensured that the United Nations lacks such capability, reflecting the view of most governments (and specificly the two Superpowers) during the Cold War that the United Nations would not be permitted to play a significant independent political role in world events. What operational capability did exist was found in the essentially autonomous agencies such as the U.N. High Commissioner for Refugees, the U.N. Children's Fund, and the World Food Program, and is limited to their areas of expertise. Therefore, while the United Nations was capable enough to manage the essentially simple peace monitoring operations authorized up to the late 1980s (the Congo situation apart) on the one hand, and the various natural disasters or humanitarian crises on the other, the combination of the two—and at a higher level of activity—in the phenomena called "complex political emergencies" was clearly beyond the organizational and managerial competence of the U.N. as it then existed. It proved easy enough to find the troops and other field personnel, but the rapid expansion and increasing complexity of deployed U.N. peace operations quickly revealed the necessity to expand and improve the logistical and policy support mechanism in headquarters.

As the sole remaining global power was disinclined to assume global policing responsibilities, a widespread instinct surfaced in many governments to turn to the United Nations to deal with these problems. However the demands on U.N. peacekeeping capability threatened to overwhelm the system as the number of such operations doubled and their complexity increased as humanitarian and political/military considerations became intertwined. Cambodia and Iraq presented operational, not to mention political, challenges never before faced by the United Nations. Second-generation peacekeeping had arrived.

In late 1991, the General Assembly, after a year long debate, passed a resolution creating the Department of Humanitarian Affairs. In early 1992, the Security Council (in a special chief of state session) asked the Secretary-General to report back to the Council on the evolving international situation and the potential role of the United Nations. New Secretary-General Boutros Boutros-Ghali did so in his "Agenda for Peace," which laid out a more direct and active role for the United Nations in a range of conflict resolution and peace operations. The new role calls for intervention in the internal affairs of sovereign countries under certain conditions—a dramatic change in the international environment—and the concept of multifaceted U.N. peace missions involving economic, social, and human rights as well as political/military considerations.

This rapid expansion of demands on the United Nations, accepted in principle in the "Agenda for Peace," and mandated by the Security Council in specific cases such as Cambodia, quickly overwhelmed the United Nation's minimal crisis management capability. Beginning in 1989 there were demands and proposals for clarification of responsibility and fundamental organizational change in the U.N. system. Some of these were initiated by Member States (the Department of Humanitarian Affairs) and some by Boutros Boutros-Ghali. These changes assume that U.N. peacekeeping authority will remain situation specific, and not become a general authority. They also assume that crisis management in the United Nations will continue to take place at three levels in the case of U.N.-led peace operations:

- Security Council: overall political authority and policy direction
- Secretary-General: policy and executive direction
- Special Representative of the Secretary-General/Force Commander: command in the field: one, or both, in hierarchical relationship .

The reorganization process was effectively initiated by General Assembly resolution 46/182 of December 1991, which authorized a new Department of Humanitarian Affairs (DHA). DHA was created by U.N. Member States to deal with a widely shared concern about the organization's shortcomings in dealing with the explosive problem of manmade humanitarian crises (specificly the problem of poor coordination among U.N. agencies in responding to the refugee problem in northern Iraq) and the equally widely shared opinion that the existing U.N. system of autonomous organizations (UNHCR, UNICEF, WORLD FOOD PROGRAM, etc.) was not sufficiently integrated to manage them effectively. DHA began its operations in April 1992.

In January 1992 the Secretary-General began consolidating the collection of political departments described above into two departments: Political Affairs (DPA) and Peacekeeping Operations (DPKO). Most of the previous bureaucratic units were folded into DPA, except for the Division for Outer Space Affairs, which was moved to U.N. Headquarters in Vienna. At the same time, the Secretary-General announced the creation of a new Department of Peacekeeping Operations (DPKO), headed by an Under-Secretary-General and replacing the small office of Special Political Affairs located in the Secretary-General's immediate office.

These three, essentially new departments faced very different challenges. The Department of Political Affairs had to absorb and digest a mishmash of departments, programs, and units—the "flotsam and jetsam of nearly two decades of Third-World originated General Assembly politicking," as a distinguished observer of U.N. affairs put it. The Department of Peacekeeping Operations had to expand and acquire resources scattered around the Secretariat to do jobs that were in some sense an evolution of what it had been doing, but that were now bigger, faster moving, more complex, and more dangerous. The Department of Humanitarian Affairs had to start from scratch, picking up personnel and units from around the system and overcoming builtin resistance from large, well established operating agencies whose expertise was deeper and broader that the new department.

Implementation and Effectiveness

This period of organizational innovation, change, and reform that began in 1991 continues today with opinion as to its efficacy to date ranging from a "good beginning" to "marginal at best." All these efforts are still essentially in the developmental stage, and implementation is taking place concurrently with actual operations in a very fluid international environment. Insider opinions vary as to the success to date of interdepartmental integration and coordination and in all fairness it is probably too early to make judgements. Some improvements are, nevertheless, already noticeable. DPKO is certainly a more robust organization (especially on the military planning side) and DPKO/DPA/DHA coordination is happening. For instance, all field reporting from all these departments is regularly distributed now to the other departments.

The set of interdepartment managing committees (Secretary-General's Task Force, Inter-Agency Standing Committee, etc.) are very active, producing a sort of meeting mania, and appear to be accomplishing their purpose of integrating overall management. The inclusion of several important nongovernmental organizations (NGOs) on the IASC is an important innovation, which recognizes the importance of UN-National Government-NGO cooperation. However, it is difficult to judge the overall effect on policy, given the difficulties being faced by the major peacekeeping operations and the political turbulence surrounding the whole question of peacekeeping.

Also unclear is the competence of the newly established departmental units necessary for better and more integrated performance by the United Nations as a system: the planning, intelligence, early warning, and training units. For instance, DHA's Early Warning System and Disaster Management Training Program are both still in the developmental stage and are designed to focus only on humanitarian problems.

While interdepartmental integration appears to be making some progress, less movement is discernable with respect to U.N. programs and agencies. Given their relative autonomy, they have always been less than enthusiastic participants in combined complex-crisis operations, preferring more independent operations combined with ad hoc cooperation in the field. While they recognize the seriousness of the movement toward system integration, they remain wedded to their own historic mandates and operating culture. In specific cases, they are sometimes encouraged to do so by governments, if only because of impatience with the inadequacies of management from New York.

This situation is complicated by the Secretary-General's designation of the Administrator of UNDP as the "Coordinator to assist the Secretary-General" in managing the relief to development continuum. No one is quite sure what this means as neither the terms of this responsibility or its attendant authority has ever been spelled out, but it confuses the image of an integrated effort to manage complex emergencies by introducing the question of development, which is clearly outside the mandates of DPA/DPKO/DHA and by introducing another coordinator of humanitarian activities. Given all these developments, it is not surprising that the specialized agencies are moving very cautiously. They have formulated the criterion of added value and are asking how any of these new arrangements would provide such.

One still unresolved question is the degree to which U.N. Member States wish to create a permanent crisis management capability in U.N. Headquarters. While DPA and DHA have, more or less, regular budgets and staffing allocations, DPKO is essentially an ad hoc organization whose size and funding are reflections of ongoing peacekeeping operations. Therefore, if, for instance, UNPROFOR were to be closed down, the very sizable contribution to the Peacekeeping Support Account from the UNPROFOR budget would end. This means that DPKO's institutional role—memory, lessons learned, mission and doctrine planning, etc.—is at the mercy of current operations.

Another aspect of this question is the degree to which this augmentation of U.N. crisis management capability is dependent upon voluntary donations from Member States. Almost all the present military staff in DPKO (94 out of 118 on duty in U.N. Headquarters) are on loan from Member States. Various governments have made and are making contributions in kind, ranging from expert teams to design the new organization and processes (for instance, the U.S. Government's Logistics Working Group) to Swedish communications equipment. Some countries are also making cash contributions, such as the British Governments one-time donation of £1.6 million in January 1995 to the Department of Humanitarian Affairs for the enhancement of complex emergency coordination and rapid response to complex emergencies. At some point, Member States may wish to review the total budget for crisis management and decide at what permanent level they wish to fund it.

In sum, the Secretary-General, supported by General Assembly resolutions, has launched an organizational reform of the United Nations to provide for greater integration and coordination of constituent U.N. bodies in the management of complex emergencies—humanitarian, peacekeeping, or a mixture. Three new departments have been created, staffed, and placed into a dynamic relationship to serve as the Secretary-General's crisis-management staff. In the short run, this process is having mixed results, adding to the United Nations' well-known propensity for bureaucracy while creating new capabilities and interdepartmental relations, which promise greater competence in the future. The implications of these changes when they reach fruition for Member States in general and countries involved in a particular crisis situation are obvious. At present, Member States will have to resist the temptation of cynicism and short-term expedients in order to support this process if they want the United Nations of the future to perform better than the United Nations of today.

II. The Triad:
The New Departments

By mid-1994 the respective roles of the three "crisis management" departments were clearly identified. Hereafter called the Triad, they were to constitute a crisis-management and coordinating structure for the Secretary-General, covering political and military conflicts and humanitarian crises:

- DPA is the "political" department, dealing with ongoing political relations and questions.
- DPKO is the mission planner and operator, mobilized in each case by a specific mandate from the Security Council.
- DHA is the coordinator of the U.N. system's "civilian" agencies when they are called upon to work in a multidiscipline emergency situation (either purely humanitarian or complex political emergency situation).

Despite this generally accepted clarity of department "missions," jurisdictional problems continue to exist, especially between DPA and DPKO.

Together with the Department of Administration and Management (which remains responsible for procurement) and the Office of the Legal Advisor, these departments constitute the "crisis manager" staff of the United Nations (figure 1).

Department of Political Affairs
The decentralized character of the United Nations was especially notable in the political area where, by the end of the 1980s, four Under-Secretaries General and numerous Assistant Secretary-Generals in six distinct departments jostled for roles in the U.N. Headquarters New York:

- Department for Political and General Assembly Affairs
- Department for Political and Security Council Affairs
- Department for Disarmament Affairs
- Office for Special Political Affairs
- Centre Against Apartheid
- Division of Outer Space Affairs
- Office for Research and the Collection of Information (ORCI).

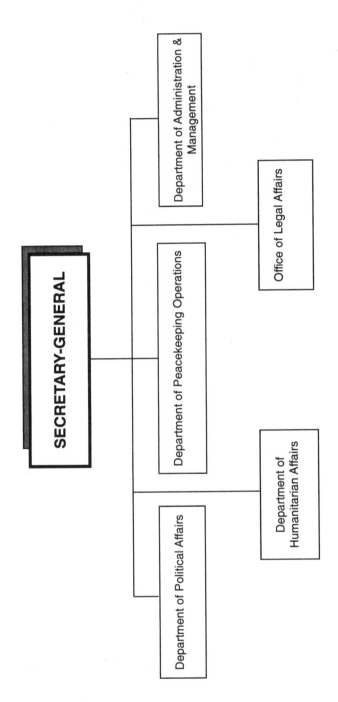

Figure 1. United Nations Secretariat

DPA was created by merging five of the departments on the above list: the Division of Outer Space Affairs was kept separate and moved to Vienna, and the Office for Special Political Affairs became the nucleus of the new Department for Peacekeeping Operations. Initially the DPA was headed by a pair of Under-Secretaries General who divided up the political work on geographic lines. (The establishment of a duumvriate management arose out of complicated historical reasons involving both personalities and the competition for senior U.N. jobs among Member States.) When one of these Under-Secretary-Generals retired in 1993, the reorganization of the department was able to move ahead under the more normal arrangement calling for a single department head. The present structure was confirmed and put into place by the end of 1994 (figure 2).

DPA is the primary pre-crisis political operator in the U.N. system and the regular pipeline to the Secretary-General on political matters. It performs U.N. regular diplomatic work and is generally responsible for identification and analysis of developing political crises. To accomplish this objective, DPA is being equipped with new communications and computing equipment and being operationally integrated with the rest of the U.N. system, especially its fellow crisis managers, DPKO and DHA.

Apart from substantive political work, DPA was made responsible for providing staff support for the Security Council, the General Assembly, the Trusteeship Council and related subordinate intergovernmental bodies (interpreters, translators, secretariat staff, etc). It also includes an Electoral Assistance Division, which provides assistance on referendums and elections. This unit, a major innovation in the United Nations, was the creation of the General Assembly on the initiative of mostly Western governments desirous of equipping the United Nations to assist the growth of democratically elected governments in the post-Cold War world. It was originally placed in DPA, moved briefly to DPKO, and then returned to DPA.

DPA staff totals 350. Of its personnel, approximately one third serve as secretariat support for the Security Council, the General Assembly, the Trusteeship Council, and other intergovernmental bodies. An additional number perform specialized duties such as Charter research and Military Staff Committee Secretariat. A certain number occupy themselves with specialized matters such as disarmament, Palestinian questions, and decolonization. The rest function as desk officers much in the manner of staff officers in foreign affairs ministries. They are organized into regional offices, divided between two Assistant Secretary-Generals.

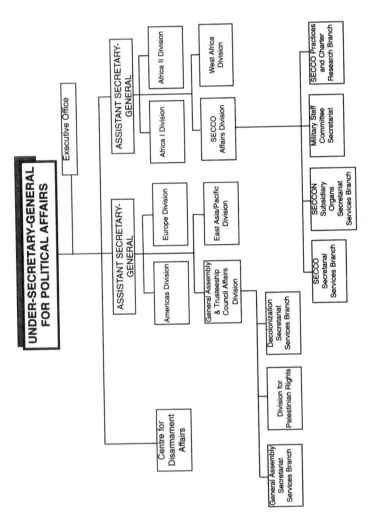

Figure 2. Department of Political Affairs

The department's proposed program budget (regular and extrabudgetary) for the biennium 1996-97 is $66.6 million, of which $50.0 million is for the operational programs. This is a significant decline from the early 1990s, reflecting the end of various programs in Southern Africa. On the other hand, there have been increases in preventive diplomacy, disarmament, and electoral assistance (appendix B).

The Department of Peacekeeping Operations (DPKO)

DPKO was created in 1992, replacing the Office for Special Political Affairs. According to its Organization Manual, the Department is "responsible for the planning, preparation, conduct, and direction of all U.N. field operations, in particular peace-keeping operations, and assists in the provision of substantive services to the Security Council and the General Assembly; it provides secretarial services to the Special Committee on Peace-keeping Operations." DPKO'S new structure and expanded staff illustrates the distinction between traditional and contemporary peacekeeping—a multidisciplinary activity where U.N. military and political peacekeepers, Blue Beret and others, are teamed with civilian experts in fields ranging from electoral assistance to caring for refugees.

DPKO's current organization fell into place in 1994 after a good deal of turmoil and unplanned expansion following its creation in 1992 (figure 3 and appendix C). It is essentially composed of three major elements: The Office of the Under-Secretary-General, the Office of Planning and Support, and the Office of Operations. In addition to the functions and capabilities taken over from previously existing organizations (e.g., the Military Advisor, field operations), DPKO now includes a number of new functions and offices (Situation Centre, civilian police and demining units, etc.).

DPKO's new structure strengthens the office of the USG by incorporating the Office of the Military Advisor and including the Situation Centre and a Policy and Analysis Unit. This last unit is responsible for studying peacekeeping policy issues and operations and codifying lessons learned. The body of the department is divided into two major divisions, each headed by an Assistant Secretary-General: one for Planning and Support, the other for Operations. These two Assistant Secretary-General-led organizations provide a functional alignment and span of control effectiveness previously lacking in peacekeeping operations.

The Office of Operations is organized geographicly with desk officers for each peacekeeping mission who coordinate the day-to-day executive

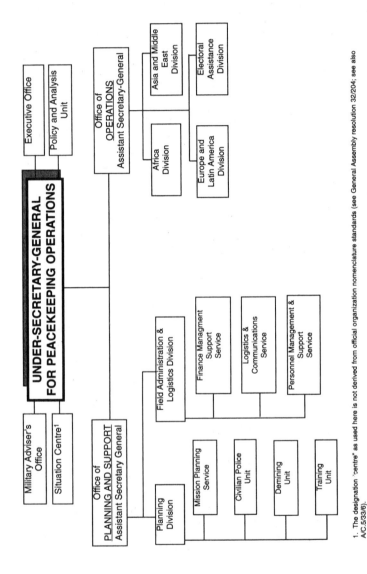

Figure 3. Department of Peacekeeping Operations

1. The designation "centre" as used here is not derived from official organization nomenclature standards (see General Assembly resolution 32/204; see also A/C.5/33/6).

direction of peacekeeping operations and other field missions. The Office of Planning and Support is divided into two major divisions. Planning Division includes Mission Planning Services, Civilian Police, Demining, and Training units. The Field Administration and Logistics Division is the old Field Operations Division from the Department of Administration and Management, which was transferred to DPKO in 1993. It provides the "care and feeding" of peacekeeping missions: financial management, logistics, communications, and personnel management services.

The growth of U.N. staff managing peacekeeping operations in the U.N. headquarters rose dramatically from 1991 to 1995. The Office of Special Political Affairs had a total staff of about three dozen, of whom only three were military officers. In addition, there was the Field Operations Division of the Department of Administration and Management, which provided the headquarters logistical planning and support, with a staff of about 60. DPKO's staff now totals approximately 420, of which about 100 are military officers on loan from their governments. As the recruiting of a permanent military staff was not envisaged, DPKO is dependant on the willingness of Member States to lend experienced officers, and current staffing arrangements are based on the assumption that Member States would make officers available, both on regular assignments in headquarters and on special assignments in specific emergencies. Several governments (including the United States) have already provided military personnel on short-term assignments (and at no cost to the United Nations) and others are lining up to do so.

DPKO as a department has a proposed budget of US $128.4 million for the binennium 1996-97. This amount provides for all headquarters operations, two peacekeeping missions (UNTSO and UNMOGIP), and the Office of the U.N. Special Coordinator in the Occupied Territories, all funded from the regular budget. The 1996-97 proposed budget cannot include, obviously, any provisions for ad hoc missions undertaken at the request of the Security Council, the General Assembly, governments, or at the initiative of the Secretary-General in the exercise of his good offices role. Yet the 1994-1995 budget includes a sum of almost $50 million for such missions, and it is reasonable to assume that similiar missions will be requested and mounted during the course of the biennium (appendix D).

These funds are distinct from the 18 U.N. peacekeeping operations, apart from the two mentioned above, which are covered in separate peacekeeping operations budgets authorized by the Security Council and the General Assembly. The cost of U.N. peacekeeping operations in 1994 was $3.5 billion (appendix E).

Department of Humanitarian Affairs

DHA was created by General Assembly resolution 46/182 as a coordinating organization. It has a double mandate: to function as the inter-agency coordinator in specific crises, and to foster a general "climate of cooperation" among U.N. funds, programs, and agencies. Its first 2 years was notable for the criticism from all sides, including a number of major governments. Interdepartmental coordination is inherently difficult and tends to be resisted by the existing bureaucratic organs, in this case the political departments and the U.N. operating programs and specialized agencies. Some governments were also leery at first, especially those who had been concerned that a U.N. Department of Humanitarian Affairs implied a new interventionist United Nations. DHA's effort to coordinate also ran into problems as governments had difficulty adjusting to the new system, for example, by continuing to pledge funds to individual agency appeals rather than waiting for DHA'S combined appeal program.

Organized in 1992 DHA was an organizational hodge-podge until completely restructured in late 1994. It has suffered from the usual startup problems, which were exacerbated by being pushed into operations from its first day of existence and a growing demand for its services. It should be noted that DHA is built upon a previously existing natural disaster organization located in Geneva (U.N. Disaster Relief Organization, UNDRO), and thus began life as, and continues to be, a bifurcated organization with two headquarters offices. Adjustment of this geographical division (stemming from history and reinforced by inter-governmental politics), expansion of the role, reorganization of the functions, and integration of a disparate staff of varying quality and background have been difficult tasks (appendix F).

The current organization consolidated the existing geographic desk officers in New York and Geneva into a single Complex Emergency Division centered in New York (figure 4). The Under-Secretary-General for Humanitarian Affairs and his personal staff—DHA's Executive Office—is located in New York.

The operating units of DHA are divided into two Offices, one in New York and one in Geneva (although the NY Office also has one unit—the Complex Emergency Support Unit—physically located in Geneva).

• DHA's New York Office itself is divided into two major operating units. The Complex Emergency Division is composed of geographic desk officers who focus on humanitarian diplomacy, ongoing operations including initial response to an emergency, and relations with other U.N. organizations. The Policy Analysis Division does

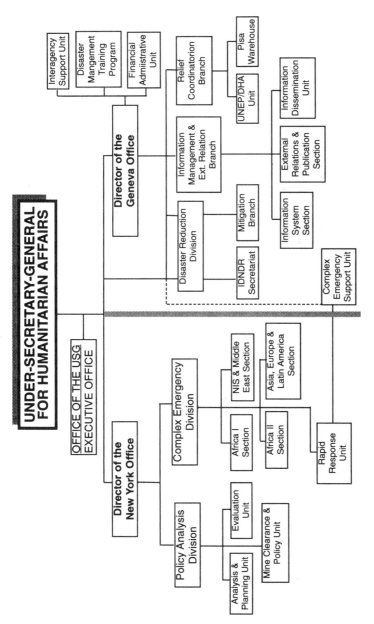

Figure 4. Department of Humanitarian Affairs

policy and program evaluation, including managing HEWS, and runs the demining program.

• DHA's Geneva Office assumed the operations of the former U.N. Disaster Relief Organization (UNDRO) and focuses on implementation of programs, operational coordination, logistical support, financial administration, training, and information management, with particular concentration on mitigation and response to natural disasters. (In this effort it is supported by the Secretariat of the International Decade on Natural Disaster Reduction - a special General Assembly auuthorized program).

In addition to its operational units, DHA is responsible for chairing or coordinating a number of interagency committees and programs, specificly the Inter-Agency Standing Committee (IASC), the Central Emergency Revolving Fund (CERF), and the Humanitarian Early Warning System (HEWS).

As of mid-1995, the department has a staff of 210, 69 based in New York and the rest in Geneva. Its annual regular budget is approximately $10 million ($19 million authorized for 1994-95 biennium; $20.3 million request for 1996-97). An additional $12-15 million per year is transferred from extra-budgetary resources of $145 million to cover headquarters staff and activities directly related to or stemming from specific programs. Extra-budgetary resources refers to special, substantive activities—as in Afghanistan, Cambodia, Rwanda, and general disaster relief— authorized by the General Assembly, and financed by special trust funds managed by DHA (appendix G).

III. Capabilities and Functions

The organizational reform of the Triad is intended to provide the United Nations with a toolbox of management capabilities that combine to provide the organization with an enhanced ability to mount and manage multilateral missions dealing with complex political and humanitarian emergencies. The major capabilities envisaged are:

- Mission planning
- Early warning
- Communications
- Situation center
- Information collation and distribution
- Rapid response
- Standby arrangements
- Logistics and procurement reform
- Financial appeal process
- Training
- Services to governments
- Mission evaluation

Some of these capabilities have long existed in the U.N. system, but in a fairly embryonic state nevertheless sufficient for the management demands placed on the United Nations by "traditional" peacekeeping. An earlier attempt to equip the United Nations with emergency management capability in the politically neutral area of natural emergencies achieved only modest success. UNDRO (U.N. Disaster Relief Organization) was established in the early 1970s and located in Geneva, but its perceived failure to live up to expectations was one of the reasons for the movement to create the DHA in 1991. Up to very recently, U.N. communications were extremely primitive by contemporary national standards, and U.N. peacekeeping missions in the field knew that rapid (e.g., telephonic) contact was an ad hoc arrangement. Mission planning was a sometime thing, undertaken without designated staff or financial resources largely on the margins of the negotiations leading to any specific Security Council mandate.

The organizational innovations and changes of the past 3 years have focused on enhancing where possible or creating where necessary these capabilities. Obviously, as of the end of 1995, this is an uncompleted process and the following comments are intended to provide an overview of these developments.

Mission Planning

The Mission Planning Service of DPKO was established to provide planning capability for peacekeeping operations from conception to withdrawal. A formal planning capability for field missions is an innovation for the United Nations; traditional peacekeeping missions were planned on the back of an envelope, so to speak, as delegates negotiated the relevant Security Council mandate. That procedure was adequate for traditional type missions, but Mission Planning Service was created to deal with the more complicated, multidimensional role of most if not all present-day operations, to include interdepartmental coordination with DHA and U.N. humanitarian assistance, human rights, and related activities.

Mission Planning Service's first major task was to prepare a detailed plan for UNAVEM III. On an ongoing basis, Mission Planning, working with FALD, is concentrating on standardizing procedures by developing "mission templates," a Survey Mission Handbook, and a Standard Costs Manual. The mission templates and Survey Mission Handbook will outline the basic requirements an operational assumptions for operations of various sizes and mandates and will provide the guidelines and requirements for planning and mounting a specific new peace operation. It will also attempt to identify, codify, and distribute "lessons learned" in specific operations. A discrete function of Mission Planning is the establishment and maintenance of a system of national standby forces and other capabilities that interested Member States maintain at an agreed state of readiness as a possible contribution to U.N. peacekeeping operations.

The United States is assisting Mission Planning Service by sending U.S. military logistics experts to New York to work with the DPKO Field Administration and Logistics Division, to prepare generic guidelines, manuals, and SOPs on operational logistics, budgeting, and contracting as well as assistance in mounting specific ongoing U.N. operations.

Early Warning

The major U.N. agencies always had their own individual data bases and some form, albeit usually quite informal, of an early-warning system. With the growing number of complex emergencies and the consequent demand on available resources, interest in a systemwide data base and early-warning system developed. Two U.N. agencies have now developed their own formal early warning systems:

- UNEP: GEMS (Global Environmental Monitoring Survey)
- FAO: GIEWS (Global Information and Early Warning System)

Others are in the process of defining and creating similar systems relevant to their areas of concern: WHO to monitor communicable disease developments, and UNHCR to watch for dramatic shifts in population movements.

Pending installation of the UNHCR early warning system, a special series of "Consultations on Early Warning of New Flows of Refugees and Displaced Persons" were started in 1993, initiated by the ACC Ad Hoc Working Group on that subject. The Consultations are organized and chaired by DHA and include as regular participants UNHCR, FAO, UNICEF, UNDP, UNEP, UNESCO, WHO, WFP, IOM, ICRC and DPA. They are held every 6 to 8 weeks and are responsible for producing an interagency report to the Under-Secretary-General for DHA for onward transmission to the IASC as the senior policy level specifically charged with managing humanitarian crises and then to interested parties throughout the U.N. system. The Consultation group is charged with both collating early warning on refugee flows and proposals for action. Although NGOs, academic specialists, and government representatives have been invited to the Consultations, few have yet accepted. Consideration is being given to making selected outsiders regular members of the talks instead of ad hoc invitees.

DHA began designing its own Humanitarian Early Warning System (HEWS) in summer of 1993. It is intended to compile and analyze information from several and varied sources with the purpose of identifying potential crises with humanitarian implications. By January 1995, DHA staff completed a prototype country early warning format, which includes a database, trend evaluation, and analysis process. DHA had created approximately 100 country profiles by late spring 1995 and planned to produce the first country assessment by mid-1995.

HEWS draws upon the existing U.N. system of organizations including the Bretton Woods institutions, international and inter-governmental organizations, NGOS, and public information sources as well as the existing agency warning systems and databases mentioned above. HEWS database includes various quantitative indicators as well as qualitative information gather from a variety of sources, graphical trends evaluation, and analyses generated by the application of neutral network techniques. Updated continually, it will generate products such as country profiles, and regional summaries, and trend analyses. Defined critical factors will be monitored for changes and, when necessary, used to produce early warning signals. The HEWS system will produce periodic general reports, early warning signals, followup reports, country profiles, maps, and other products (written and Internet) as necessary. These products are designed to be readily available for retrieval by DHA desk officers and other relevant staff within the U.N. Secretariat, especially DPA and DPKO desk officers.

Of wider scope is the proposal for an electronic information-sharing system, using the INTERNET, for humanitarian operations. To be called ReliefWeb, it will be managed by DHA, and HEWS will be a contributor. Relief Net is being co-sponsored by various governments, including the USG, NGOs such as Interaction, and the International Council of Voluntary Agencies (ICVA)in Geneva. DHA has hired a project manager to set it up with the intention to have it in operation by the end of the year. Relief Net will deal strictly with information, not analysis or predictions, and will be designed to serve as a data base and an early warning system for the global humanitarian assistance community.

Situation Centre

The Situation Centre was established as part of DPKO headquarters in New York in April 1993, where it is attached directly to the office of the Under-Secretary-General for Peacekeeping Operations and consists of two components, the Duty Room and the Information and Research Unit (I&R) (appendix H). The Situation Centre has a staff of 27 professionals, most of whom are military/civilian officers on temporary assignment from their governments.

The Duty Room is a communications center manned as a 24-hour point of contact to facilitate communications and the information flow between New York and DPKO's peacekeeping missions. It monitors all current peacekeeping operations (and provide 24-hour, 7 days a week field communications) and provides information briefs to DPKO senior staff.

The Centre's Information and Research Unit (I&R) prepares daily situation briefings and information summaries based on field reports, open source publications, and information provide by member governments. I&R was originally established as a point of contact to which Member States could pass sanitized intelligence information. Now its function is three-fold: to receive and disseminated intelligence at the U.N. Restricted level from Member States that contribute to the management of and decisionmaking about peacekeeping operations, to respond to requests for intelligence from staff members of DPKO (including field missions), and to help establish a basic intelligence function within the department. These efforts are still in an early stage and include the preparation of information security guidelines for the

Department and field missions (although not a classification system as stringent as many countries).

However, as the very word "intelligence" is traditionally anathema in the U.N. community, most information gathering and management is still from open-source material, although that situation is being modified by the provision of operation specific "intelligence" information from various national governments. While questions have been raised as to the possibility and desirability of a U.N. "controlled or classified" source information system, nothing has been instituted yet beyond a basic "U.N. Restricted" classification. To facilitate the transfer of information from governments, the United Nations has purchased the Joint Deployable Intelligence Support system, a sophisticated computer that provides for the transfer of U.N. restricted information directly from governments to the Situation Centre. Most analysis is still of the type done by desk officers and senior officials as part of their operational duties, and little has been done yet to design and negotiate an information protocol to deal with more sensitive material dealing with analysis, intelligence gathering and reporting, and copyrighted material.

DHA does not have its own situation or communications center in New York, where it views itself as a customer of the Situation Centre, especially for communciating with political missions in the field. DHA instituted (spring 1995) a 24-hour duty-officer system for its New York staff, reachable either through the Situation Centre or directly through a commercial beeper system. DHA does have its own situation room in Geneva for purely natural disasters.

Communications

Prior to these changes, the United Nations in general, and Office of Special Political Affairs in particular, lacked a modern command, control, and communications system. After deciding on a bureaucratic structure (Situation Centre, etc.) DPKO asked the U.S. Government to conduct a study of its needs in this area. The United States sent a 10-person expert working group to provide a detailed proposal for a modern communications architecture using commercial off-the-shelf technology that would provide DPKO with modern command control capability and facilitate interoperability with the major contributors to peacekeeping operations. The report, forwarded in December 1994, estimates the cost of implementation at US $40 million, which the United Nations intends to finance out of existing budgets. However, progress in the estimated 24-month implementation schedule has been slow.

DHA has also been involved in efforts to strengthen, integrate and rationalize its information management and telecommunications system.

In early 1994 it drew up and adopted an information management strategy. First step in implementing this strategy was to accept an offer by the Office of Foreign Disaster Assistance of USAID to finance a local area computer network, to include both equipment and software, for slightly over $300,000, for delivery by 1995. This network will enable DHA integrate its internal communications and information and interact with other relevant departments. It replaces an inadequate collection of stand-alone computers.

DHA then began planning for the creation of a dedicated information platform for the use of the international humanitarian assistance community (ReliefWeb). As a third step, DHA in early 1994 asked the United States to conduct a study of its total communications and information needs similar to that being done for DPKO. The U.S. Government has agreed to provide this study for completion by 1995.

DHA maintains its own small stocks of standby telecommunications equipment (IMARSAT A and M, high-frequency radios, and walkie-talkie sets) for use in initial emergency deployments. It recently formalized a standby agreement with the Swedish Rescue Services Agency for a range of standby telecommunications equipment and communications specialist staff up to the largest size of currently existing in-country DHA coordination unit (the U.N. Rwanda Emergency Office.)

Information Collation and Distribution

The United Nations itself has always produced a great deal of relevant information with respect to developing crises and to ongoing operations: demographic, geographic, population movements, weather, agriculture, health conditions, food supply, transport systems, social, economic, and political conditions, and the security situation, to mention the most obvious. However, much of this information is gathered or produced by and for U.N. agencies and departments pursuant to their individual mandates, for example, Food and Agriculture Organization and rural economic conditions and food supplies. The well known "stovepipe" structure of the U.N. (that is, largely autonomous bureaucracies that interact only at the most senior level, if at all) has inhibited the pooling and sharing of this information for early-warning and crisis-management purposes.

Pending the development of a U.N.-wide data base, this information remains buried in the individual agencies, although some compilation is traditionally made in UNDP country program reports. (An earlier attempt at a system wide database by the Office for Research and Collection of Information [ORCI] did not move much beyond planning for such a data base and early warning system.) In the past few years, there has been much talk about the concept of "Information Focal Points." It is not yet clear whether this means the creation of specific units or offices. Meanwhile an information collation, exchange, and distribution process within the Triad is in the early stages of being created. It has two elements.

The three Departments of the Triad are organizing and conducting an information exchange system among their desk officers by which they call together each other for pre-crisis consultations when the situation appears to call for it. In support of this process, a file of "information packets" will be prepared for distribution among the participants. These packets will contain a specially prepared situation report, security updates, and situation summary, plus whatever else is available (U.N. agency reports plus open source material such as FBIS reports, newspaper clippings, etc). DPKO's Information and Research Unit (I&R) is a major contributor to these packets.

The Triad is conducting a series of six "simulation exercises" involving officials from various departments to prepare these country packets. The first two of these country meetings were conducted in early 1995. The first meeting concentrated on Burundi and a 34-page packet was prepared by the "Framework" team. The rest of these "simulation" exercises were planned for completion in 1995, with continued experimentation on the contents and format of the packets expected. For the moment, the packets contain only collected material, without analysis. Concurrently, I&R is designing an electronic country profile system, in conjunction with an interdepartmental information-sharing network.

Meanwhile, various governments are providing information on peace operations directly to DPKO and discussions are underway to regularize this process. For instance, the United Nations has purchased the Joint Deployable Intelligence Support system, a sophisticated computer that provides for the transfer of unclassified information directly to the U.N. Situation Centre.

Rapid Response

Initial response by the United Nations to an emergency (actual or developing) can now take several forms. The simplest and easiest is the holding of consultations among desk officers of the concerned departments, which, it is hoped, arose out of the working of the early-warning system(s). Any desk officer can convoke such a meeting, which can initiate a whole series of actions by their departments individual or the system as a whole.

Generally, the first action is the authorization and despatch of a survey team, either a DPA sponsored Initial Survey Assessment Teams, essentially designed to survey and report on the political/military aspects of a situation, or a DHA sponsored Inter-Agency Assessment Mission focused on the scope and needs of a humanitarian emergency. These teams can be sent out individually, in series, or, as is often the case, combined. Authorization for the dispatch of these teams can be done at the departmental level for humanitarian missions, but not political, although the Secretary-General is usually at least informed in advance.

It is now an accepted principal within the United Nations that sizable complex emergencies call for the appointment of a U.N. Humanitarian Coordinator in-country. This person may be either the existing U.N. Resident Coordinator or another person appointed by the Emergency Relief Coordinator (the Under-Secretary-General for Humanitarian Affairs) in consultation with other members of the Inter-Agency Coordinating Committee (IASC). The appointment of a Humanitarian Coordinator is governed by three documents approved by the IASC in December 1994: terms of reference for humanitarian coordinators, agreement to create a roster of potential coordinators, and agreement on a job profile for candidates.

Prior to the creation of DHA, its predecessor, UNDRO, focused primarily on response to natural disasters. DHA has subsequently looked into how many of the mechanisms used for natural disasters might also be applied, and modified as necessary, for complex emergencies. These include the use of standby personnel (emergency management experts) provided by donor governments (U.N. Disaster Assessment and Coordination Teams, UNDAC) who can leave within hours of a disaster to work with local authorities to carry out assessment and coordination on a disaster site, and the capacity to provide certain relief items via flights from the DHA Pisa warehouse.

UNDAC was established in 1993, and in its first year of existence was deployed to 13 natural emergencies. As a result of this experience, DHA decided to expand the UNDAC system. It has a current membership of 41 experts from 12 countries, including eleven DHA staff. Two training courses for UNDAC participants and cooperating organizations such as the International Federation of Red Cross and Red Crescent Societies and the European Commission Humanitarian Office(ECHO) have been held. A regional UNDAC for Latin America is in the process of being created for which a special training course was held in Quito in June 1995.

Current emergency management planning includes building on the experience of DHA and other U.N. humanitarian agencies working with the military of donor governments in natural disasters to developing mechanisms for their involvement in complex emergencies. An interagency working group of the U.N. humanitarian agencies was created to work with Western military representatives on this question (see following section).

DHA created its own Rapid Response Unit (RRU) in September 1994. It is a modest unit, with only four professional staff. RRU's basic function is to strengthen (or create if necessary) the coordination components of U.N. humanitarian operations in the initial emergency response phase. RRU staff themselves serve as core standby staff for quick field deployment, but their main function is building up DHA overall rapid response capacity, including the communications and standby capacities described below.

Another important innovation with respect to rapid response mechanisms is the Central Emergency Revolving Fund (CERF) by which U.N. New York can provide funds immediately to enable a U.N. agency to begin emergency relief operations without waiting until it can raise new funds from donor countries (see section titled Financial Appeal Process).

Standby Arrangements

The dramatic increase in demands on the United Nations to deal with various types of political and humanitarian crises has seriously overloaded the organization's resources (in-house or those traditionally available from Member States). Recognizing the seriousness of this problem, Secretary-General Boutros-Ghali included in his Agenda for Peace (1992) a call for systemized standby arrangements "by which governments commit themselves to hold ready, at an agreed period of notice, specially trained units for peacekeeping service." The United Nations has since concluded standby force agreements with approximately 50 Member States, including the United States; each has pledged to make military forces or equipment available for future peace operations. These commitments are for capabilities, not any specific units. The potential contributors, in addition, obviously reserve the right to reject such calls by the Security Council so the standby agreements do not provide for a ready force.

The United Nations has taken some steps to move away from the practice of funding peacekeeping operations incrementally and towards having a "reserve" fund from which to draw upon rapidly. An initial peacekeeping reserve fund has been established at a modest level to enable initial planning and mobilization. However peacekeeping budgets are specific to each operation as authorized by Member States and they are likely to continue to keep a close watch on U.N. peacekeeping operations by this control of the purse.

Additional standby arrangements are the process of being developed for specialized equipment and services. For instance, the U.N. Disaster Relief Organization (now part of DHA) has long established standby arrangements with a number of governments to provide assistance in natural disasters, like the Bangladeshi floods of several years ago. DHA is working with other relevant U.N. agencies to expand this collaboration to complex emergencies. Following the successful deployment of Swedish support services in Rwanda, DHA established a standby arrangement with the Swedish Rescue Services Agency for telecommunications, transport, logistics, and office setup support for DHA in-country coordination efforts. DHA is also revising its agreement with the Norwegian Refugee Council for NRC to add a standby capacity to its present staffing support arrangement, and is developing a similar agreement with the Russian Government ministry handling emergencies (EMERCOM) for staffing and logistics support. DHA initiated its Use of Military and Civil Defense Assets in Disaster Relief (MCDA) project in 1992 to expand this arrangement. Procedures and guidelines (the Oslo Guidelines) were elaborated for the use of these assets in such emergencies.

In response to the overwhelming needs of many hundreds of thousands of Rwandans who fled to Zaire in July 1994, UNHCR requested the assistance of governments in providing self-contained assistance packages for the key sectors. These "service packages" involved the use of resources from a multinational service package already provided for UNHCR in the Sarajevo airlift operation. UNHCR then undertook a study of the concept of a "Services Package" program that would provide standby arrangements for the provision of a package of air transport, logistical, and communications and other services for rapid introduction into a refugee/displaced person response operation.

As DHA'S MCDA project could have applicability beyond natural and technological emergencies, and UNHCR'S experience with service packages in humanitarian operations might have wider relevance for the U.N. system, a task force chaired by DHA was established in early 1995. It was charged with developing a common framework to ensure the most effective use of military and defense assets in support of all types of humanitarian operations where their use is appropriate. Specifically, the task force was to design arrangements which will provide governments with a focal point within the U.N. system, which will allow interagency priorities to be set, and which will avoid introducing any layers between users and providers of assets during an operation. The task force comprises representatives of DPKO, UNDP, UNHCR, UNICEF, WFP, and WHO and consulted with interested governments and NGOs. Its report was due to be released in late 1995.

Logistics and Procurement Reform

The transfer of FOD to DPKO was a desirable move but still did not deal with the felt necessity to reform U.N. logistic and procurement procedures. At the request of the United Nations, the United States provided a Logistics Working Group which produced a manual of recommendations in September 1993. Many of these recommendations, especially those dealing with logistics procedures and budget planning, have been adopted by the Field Administration and Logistics Division (FALD), which in early 1995 asked for a followup study to review progress.

However, U.N. procurement arrangements remain unchanged, although the subject of much debate and study. In addition to the recommendations of the U.S. Logistics Working Group, the United Nations organized a high-level Expert Procurement Group in December 1994 which produced recommendations for changes in the U.N. procurement system. However resistance to these proposals has been strong. It should be noted that procurement authority for peacekeeping operations remains in the Department of Administration and Management, and has not been transferred to DPKO.

As a practical innovation, DPKO established a logistical base and storage depot in Brindisi, Italy to provide stability and continuity to U.N. peacekeeping operations. At Brindisi, the United Nations is building mission equipment sets to expedite launching of future missions as well as equipment refurbishment capability to extend the service life of U.N. equipment. This depot provides DPKO with some (if not more) of the capability which DHA obtains from its Pisa humanitarian assistance depot.

Financial Appeal Process

Prior to the creation of DHA individual U.N. agencies would make separate appeals for funds to deal with a given emergency, despite an earlier attempt to have UNDRO coordinate a consolidated appeal process. DHA is specificly charged to do better, using two tools. It has been given the management of a $50 million revolving fund (Central Emergency Revolving Fund, CERF) and authority to concentrate the individual agencies' requests into a consolidated appeal; both procedures are now in operation.

The CERF was designed to provide U.N. emergency humanitarian relief organizations (such as UNHCR) with a "ready cash" window where they could quickly obtain the cash to initiate an emergency operation, on the assumption that most agencies had their annual budgets tied up in ongoing programs. It is set up as a revolving fund, where withdrawals will be reimbursed after the borrower(s) draws up and distributes a special appeal for the specific operation. The CERF was funded (1992) at U.S. $50 million and since then has made advances of almost $115 million and has been reimbursed almost $97 million. As of mid-April 1995, after accounting for some interest earnings, the CERF has a balance of $32 million available for use (appendix I).

The interagency consolidated appeal process, created to bring all U.N. agency resource requests for a particular complex emergency into a single appeal document, has now become an accepted procedure. This process now also typically brings together not only the U.N. humanitarian agencies but also other entities such as NGOs and the International Committee of the Red Cross into a joint review of humanitarian needs and agreement on the division of responsibility among these entities for addressing them. One problem with the regular consolidated appeals is the time required to produce them, 2 or more months. This has led DHA to take the lead in creating "flash appeals," which can be completed in 1 or 2 weeks, aimed at addressing the most urgent initial emergency response needs, pending a regular consolidated appeal.

Training

Established in 1992, the Training Unit now has a staff of 9, of whom 5 are military officers on loan from their governments. The Training Unit of DPKO comes under the direction of the Office of Planning and Support and is responsible for bringing together various previous efforts at peacekeeping training (e.g. an "SOP For Peacekeeping Operations" written 1989 prior to the establishing of DPKO) and for launching a much more ambitious program to coordinate and standardize U.N. peacekeeping training. General Assembly resolutions have provided a mandate to DPKO that states that the training of peacekeeping personnel is primarily the responsibility of Member States and that the United Nations should assist them in doing so when requested. The Training Unit will act therefore as the coordinator between the United Nations and national/regional training facilities and in concert with them develop and foster training programs with a varied program of training courses and seminars (usually in cooperation with existing national and regional facilities), drafting and dissemination of training materials, research on training methods, procedures and related peacekeeping subjects.

Its basic objective is to enhance Member States' capability to provide trained and ready peacekeeping forces to the United Nations on short notice. This is a long-term process and the Training Unit has formulated a 5-year plan (1995-1999) with the following priorities:

- Develop and maintain the U.N. Training Assistance Team (UNTAT)
- Implement an active seminar and workshop program with Member States
- Publish and maintain peacekeeping documents, including training manuals, course curricula, etc.
- Establish and maintain a data-base on Member-States' mission specific and general peacekeeping training activities
- Explore the feasibility of developing a training validation system to ensure that forces are ready and ready before deployment.

Implementation of this program for 1995 calls for four regional workshops, two seminars for UNTAT, one seminar for senior military/civilian officials, and one staff course. The majority of the financing for this program will come from various Member States sponsoring individual events.

As part of its coordination role, DPKO was instructed by the General Assembly to report on the peacekeeping training activities of U.N. Member States. It did so in December 1993 with a report on the activities of 30 U.N. members who replied to the questionnaire (A/48/708.1993) and is currently in the process of updating that report.

DHA and UNDP initiated a Disaster Management Training Program (DMTP) late 1991. DMTP has initially focused on natural disasters. There is an ongoing debated among U.N. agencies who have oversight of the DMTP regarding whether it should be extended to handle complex emergencies. This would require both a substantial increase in resources to enable a new program of workshops but more important the delicate question of holding workshops in a country which introduce the possibility of future armed conflict in that country.

Services to Governments

The primary purpose of the facilities and capabilities being installed in the Triad with respect to peacekeeping, humanitarian assistance, and complex emergency management is the development of the United Nations' own institutional competence. However a few activities also provide a definite service to Member States, either as participants in U.N. peacekeeping operations or as benefactors. Training as described above is one of these "services to governments." The two other major activities of this type are demining and civilian police, all institutionalized in units of the DPKO's Office of Planning and Support.

- Mine clearance has become and operational and humanitarian problem in many countries and has become an integral part of many U.N. peacekeeping missions. The Demining Unit was establishedin 1992 advises on mine-clearing activities and develops plans for demining programs.
- As the role of civilian police has become a component of many operations, the Civilian Police Unit was created to provide headquarters expertise and develop guidelines for the employment, conditions of service, training, and administration of civilian police in peacekeeping operations.

Mission Evaluation

Formal evaluation of U.N. peacekeeping and humanitarian assistance missions is now a regular process, albeit still in a rudimentary stage. DPKO's Lessons Learned Unit is specificly charged with analyzing and assessing operations and evaluating the results achieved and lessons learned from them. Located in DPKO's Mission Planning Service, it has a routinized "lessons learned" procedure for peacekeeping missions. DHA created an evaluation officer position in its Policy and Analysis Branch, responsible for evaluating (in cooperation with involved DHA action officers) specific humanitarian operations.

In accordance with the new cooperation mode enshrined in the "Framework for Cooperation" initiative, DPKO and DHA are under instructions to share input and analysis of their respective evaluations. DHA staff, in fact, have been active participants in recent DPKO lessons-learned seminars.

IV. Interdepartmental Relations

The United Nations has been responding to emergencies since its founding, but generally in the form of humanitarian assistance delivered by specialized agencies such as UNHCR or UNICEF. When several agencies were involved in an extensive operation, the United Nations usually utilized the "lead agency" system, for example, UNHCR in the former Yugoslavia. However the growth of more complex emergencies involving an openly political (that is, peacekeeping) element created a planning, resource, and management burden which even the most robust U.N. agencies found difficult to handle in the old manner. This was particularly a problem at the headquarters level in New York and Geneva, where the necessary integration of policy has to be done.

Member States focused quickly on the need for both more resources and better integration in responding to humanitarian crises. On the humanitarian assistance side, this led to General Assembly action to create DHA and the consolidated appeal process. On the political side, Member States pushed the Secretary-General to make changes and specificly to improve coordination, and where appropriate integration, in the U.N. system. The coordination and integration process is about money, staff, or departmental roles and about attitudes and working relations.

The resulting coordination and integration process takes place at two levels:

- Within the Secretariat (DPA, DPKO, DHA, Legal Counsel, administrative services,etc)
- Between the Secretariat and the Funds, Programs, and Agencies when they are involved.

Committees and Task Forces

To obtain this improved coordination, the Secretary-General has created a network of committees and task forces:

Secretary-General's Task Force on U.N. Operations
Chaired by the Secretary-General, meets weekly, composed of six Secretariat Under-Secretary-Generals (DPA, DPKO, DHA,

DAM, and two of the Secretary-General's senior political advisors) plus the Legal Counsel; responsible for general policy, and direction of specific peacekeeping operations.

Under-Secretaries' Meeting

DPA, DPKO, DHA: meets ad hoc to discuss organizational coordination.

Inter-Agency Standing Committee (IASC)

An inter-agency coordination mechanism created by the General Assembly resolution which created DHA; chaired by DHA; and composed of DHA, UNDP, UNICEF, WFP, and other programs and agencies as relevant. DPA and DPKO participate as observers as do four important non-U.N. and nongovernmental organizations:

- International Organization for Migration (IOM)
- International Committee of the Red Cross (ICRC)
- International Federation of Red Cross/Crescent Societies
- International Committee for Volunteer Agencies (ICVA)

The IASC meets 3 or 4 times annually at the Under-Secretary-General level and at least 7 or 8 times at the Working Group or deputies level. It is responsible for the coordination of the non-political and non-military activities of crisis management, including the operation of the Inter-Agency Consolidated Appeals Fund.

Inter-Agency Support Unit (IASU) is a Secretariat support unit for the IASC, composed of temporarily assigned senior officers from the relevant agencies plus an NGO representative, located in Geneva.

IASC Working Group is a form of "deputies committee" composed of senior staff from agencies represented on IASC which meets between IASC meeting to prepare the agenda and negotiate policy documents and decisions for final approval by the heads of agencies.

Peacekeeping Working Groups

Chaired by DPKO, created to manage a specific peacekeeping operation/mission (e.g. Somalia). Membership and meeting schedule determined by character of operation.

Framework for Cooperation

The creation of DHA reflected a widespread recognition of the necessary role of humanitarian and other civilian assistance programs in contemporary peace operations. Responding to that concern, the Secretary-General noted in his report on the work of the organization (A/48/1):

> The international community has asked that more be done to strengthen the capacity of the U.N. to provide humanitarian assistance, through coordinated planning and implementation involving the Departments of Political Affairs, Peacekeeping Operations, and Humanitarian Affairs, and that humanitarian concerns should be reflected in fact-finding missions and in peacekeeping operations.I have therefore taken steps to insure that essential collaboration takes place among those Departments and between them and all other U.N. organizations and bodies.

In pursuit of this commitment, the Secretary-General reorganized the headquarters departments into the Triad described above. He also issued an instruction in early 1994 which clarified the chain-of-command responsibilities of Special Representatives in the field. In this instruction, the Secretary-General laid down the rule that all special representatives heading peacekeeping operations would report to the USG for Peacekeeping Operations through a single reporting channel (DPKO) with copies to DPA and DHA. Previously such representatives had reported to various officials in New York: some to the Secretary-General directly, some to the Under-Secretary-General for Political Affairs, while others reported to the Under-Secretary-General for Peacekeeping, depending upon personal ties and shifting political winds (in other words, not all field reports were available to all departments).

Following an initiative by DHA in late 1994, the three substantive departments of the Triad developed a flowchart or actions—information sharing, consultations, and joint action—for the coordination of their activities in the planning and implementation of complex operations in the field. This process or mechanism is called the "Framework for Cooperation" and was formally promulgated as U.N. doctrine in mid-1995 and so noted in the "Report of the Secretary-General on the Work of the Organization" issued on August 22, 1995 (appendix J). It consists of the following elements:

- Planning:
  —Desk and planning officers from the three Departments will interact continuously with each

other in monitoring warning signals and participating in joint analysis and consultative meetings as appropriate, in the planning of preventive action,and humanitarian and peacekeeping missions in the field.

—The three Departments will integrate their planning/operations monitoring flow charts to indicate the level and content of staff interaction expected.

—In the pre-crisis situation, all Departments must have available the same information: country profiles, risk maps, information on indicators, early warning signals, etc. Routine monitoring of country situations will be maintained through regular information sharing at the country level.

—Initial field mission results (usually conducted by humanitarian agency field staff) will be shared by all, as well as all surveys and assessments, and joint participation in these activities will be encouraged.

—DHA, and through DHA U.N. agencies, international organizations, and NGOs, will contribute to the conduct of the DPKO technical survey, the drafting of the DPKO operational concept and the mission support concept,and will have the opportunity to review and comment upon the draft Status of Forces Agreement and the initial cost analysis.

—DPKO and DPA will be invited to contribute to relevant reports on humanitarian programs and strategies for addressing complex emergencies, including the Inter-Agency Consolidated Appeals.

- Operations:
—Interdepartmental working groups will be formed at the working level throughout an operational stage of a specific mission.

—The DPKO Situation Center will be available 24 hours for DHA use. DHA may staff one of the work stations.

—Coordination between humanitarian organizations and U.N. military operations in the field will be effected through the Humanitarian Coordinator.

The motor of this interdepartmental interaction will be the ad hoc joint meetings of appropriate DPA/DPKO/DHA desk officers and/or early warning focal points of these Departments (chair to be determined by the caller) to which other Departments and Agencies will be invited as appropriate.

Appendix A
Department of Political Affairs: Mission Statement

The mission of the Department of Political Affairs (DPA) is to provide advice and support on all political matters to the Secretary-General in the exercise of his global responsibilities under the Charter relating to the maintenance of peace and security. DPA accordingly:

(a) monitors, analyzes and assesses political developments throughout the world;

(b) identifies potential or actual conflicts in whose control and resolution the United Nations could play a useful role;

(c) recommends to the Secretary-General appropriate actions in such cases and executes the approved policy;

(d) assists the Secretary-General in carrying out political activities decided by him and/or mandated by the General Assembly and the Security Council in the areas of preventive diplomacy, peace-making, peace-keeping and peace-building, including arms limitation and disarmament;

(e) provides the Secretary-General with analysis, assessment and advice on all disarmament matters and carries out the responsibilities entrusted to the Secretariat in the field of arms limitation and disarmament;

(f) provides the Secretary-General with advice on requests for electoral assistance received from Member States and coordinates implementation of programmes established in response to such requests;

(g) provides the Secretary-General with briefing materials and supports him in the political aspects of his relations with Member States;

(h) provides Secretariat services to the General Assembly, the Security Council and various of their subsidiary organs.

June 1995

Ref. MB\MISS-STA

Appendix B
Department of Political Affairs: Proposed Budget

Table 2.1   **Summary of requirements by programme**
(Thousands of United States dollars)

(1) Regular budget

Programme	1992-1993 expendi-tures	1994-1995 appropri-ations	Resource growth Amount	Resource growth Percentage	Total before recosting	Recosting	1996-1997 estimates
A. Policy-making organs	3 050.9	2 263.1	(1 239.4)	(54.7)	1 023.7	49.7	1 073.4
B. Executive direction and management	5 441.1	5 603.6	(1 753.4)	(31.2)	3 850.2	173.5	4 023.7
C. Programme of work	42 432.8	49 551.3	(1 262.5)	(2.5)	48 288.8	2 647.3	50 936.1
D. Programme support	2 768.2	4 741.7	(1 590.6)	(33.5)	3 151.1	146.2	3 297.3
Total	**53 693.0**	**62 159.7**	**(5 845.9)**	**(9.4)**	**56 313.8**	**3 016.7**	**59 330.5**

(2) Extrabudgetary resources

1992-1993 expendi-tures	1994-1995 estimates	Source of funds	1996-1997 estimates
		(a) Services in support of:	
—	—	(i) Other United Nations organizations	—
416.7	571.7	(ii) Extrabudgetary programmes	142.3
Total (a) 416.7	571.7		142.3
		(b) Substantive activities	
1 021.1	217.9	Trust Fund for the United Nations Disarmament Information Programme	233.0
194.8	390.7	Trust Fund for Public Awareness on Disarmament Issues	410.2
801.8	234.6	Trust Fund for Global and Regional Disarmament Activities	254.0
500.0	608.2	Trust Fund for Interest on the Contribution to the United Nations Special Account	400.0
208.0	6 370.4	United Nations Trust Fund for Electoral Observation	1 333.0
6.3	186.0	Trust Fund for Publicity against Apartheid	—
Total (b) 2 732.0	8 007.8		2 732.0

Source: U.N. Document A/50/6, 12 May 1995

Complex Emergencies

Section 2   **Political affairs**

1992-1993 expendi-tures	1994-1995 estimates	Source of funds	1996-1997 estimates
		(c) Operational projects	
323.5	142.3	Trust Fund for the United Nations Regional Centre for Peace and Disarmament in Africa	133.8
154.9	99.3	Trust Fund for the United Nations Regional Centre for Peace, Disarmament and Development in Latin America and the Caribbean	145.3
396.7	40.0	Trust Fund for the United Nations Regional Centre for Peace and Disarmament in Asia and the Pacific	40.0
1 433.7	2 187.3	Trust Fund for the United Nations Institute for Disarmament Research	2 187.3
4 330.0	2 130.5	United Nations Trust Fund for South Africa	—
11 138.6	5 000.0	United Nations Educational and Training Programme for Southern Africa	—
1 534.7	255.0	United Nations Fund for Namibia	—
Total (c) 19 312.1	9 854.4		2 506.4
Total (a), (b) and (c) 22 460.8	18 433.9		5 278.9
Total (1) and (2) 76 153.8	80 593.6		64 609.4

48

Appendix C

UNITED NATIONS

SECRETARIAT

ST/SGB/Organization
Section: DPKO/Amend.1
23 August 1995

ORGANIZATION MANUAL

Functions and organization of the

DEPARTMENT OF PEACE-KEEPING OPERATIONS

SECRETARY-GENERAL'S BULLETIN

95-24973 (E)

ST/SGB/Organization
Section: DPKO/Amend.1
23 August 1995

SECRETARY-GENERAL'S BULLETIN

To: Members of the staff

Subject: DEPARTMENT OF PEACE-KEEPING OPERATIONS

1.   With immediate effect, the Electoral Assistance Division has been transferred from the Department of Peace-keeping Operations to the Department of Political Affairs.

2.   Accordingly, ST/SGB/Organization, Section: DPKO is amended to reflect this change.

3.   The attached organization chart represents the amended structure of the Department of Peace-keeping Operations.

Boutros BOUTROS-GHALI
Secretary-General

Appendixes

DEPARTMENT OF PEACE-KEEPING OPERATIONS

Overview

In the context of the overall restructuring of the Secretariat, the Department of Peace-keeping Operations was created in 1992, replacing the Office for Special Political Affairs. In view of the close linkages between the Department and the Field Operations Division, the latter was incorporated into the Department in 1993 and renamed Field Administration and Logistics Division.

The Department is responsible for the planning, preparation, conduct and direction of all United Nations field operations, in particular peace-keeping operations, and assists in the provision of substantive services to the Security Council and the General Assembly; it provides secretariat services to the Special Committee on Peace-keeping Operations.

Mandate

The legislative authority for this programme of activity derives from resolutions and decisions of the Security Council and the General Assembly. The objective of the programme is the maintenance or restoration of international peace and security.

The Department serves as the operational arm of the Secretary-General for all United Nations field operations, in particular, the management and direction of peace-keeping operations. It formulates policies and procedures, based on Security Council decisions, for the establishment of new peace-keeping operations and the effective functioning of the ongoing operations; secures, through negotiations with Governments, military units and equipment as well as other military, police and civilian personnel required for peace-keeping operations; develops operational plans and methodologies for multidimensional operations, including election-monitoring; undertakes contingency planning for possible new peace-keeping operations and related activities; proposes resource requirements for these operations to the Controller for preparation and submission of budgets to the legislative bodies for approval; monitors and controls regular budget and extrabudgetary funds related to peace-keeping activities; provides logistic and administrative support for the operations in the field; maintains contacts with the parties to the conflicts and the members of the Security Council concerning the effective implementation of the Security Council's decisions; liaises with Member States, United Nations agencies and non-governmental organizations and coordinates with other entities their participation in peace-keeping operations and special missions; prepares the Secretary-General's reports to the Security Council and the General Assembly on individual peace-keeping operations and on questions of peace-keeping in general; provides

ST/SGB/Organization
Section: DPKO
Page 1
22 March 1995

substantive and secretariat services to the Special Committee on Peace-keeping Operations; and prepares training guidelines and principles for Member States.

Organizational elements and their functions

UNDER-SECRETARY-GENERAL

Performs the functions of a head of office as described in the introductory section of the *Manual* and, in addition, performs the following functions:

Directs and controls, on behalf of the Secretary-General, United Nations peace-keeping operations;

Formulates policies for peace-keeping operations and operational guidelines based on Security Council mandates;

Prepares Secretary-General's reports to the Security Council on each peace-keeping operation, with appropriate observations and recommendations;

Advises the Secretary-General on all matters related to the planning, establishment and conduct of United Nations peace-keeping missions;

Represents the Department in the meetings of the Secretary-General's Task Force on United Nations Operations;

Ensures coordination of electoral assistance projects;

Acts as a focal point between the Secretariat and Member States seeking information on all matters related to the operational and administrative aspects of peace-keeping operations.

A. Office of the Under-Secretary-General

The functions of this Office are described in the introductory section of the *Manual*. Furthermore, the Office:

Constitutes overall authority for all policies and decisions relating to the establishment and conduct of peace-keeping operations;

Appendixes

Acts as a focal point for contacts between the Secretariat and Member States, providing information on all aspects of peace-keeping operations;

Oversees the activities of the Policy and Analysis Unit, the Situation Centre 1/ and the Executive Office.

B. Military Adviser

Advises the Secretary-General, through the Under-Secretary-General for Peace-keeping Operations, on the military implications of United Nations resolutions, plans and proposals for operations in the field and advises Force Commanders on the implementation of those plans and proposals;

Provides guidance and supervision on military matters to all the military officers of the Department;

Acts as the head of the Planning Division.

C. Policy and Analysis Unit

Acts as a think-tank to provide in-depth research and analyses of emergent policy questions relevant to the areas of responsibility of the Department;

Assists the Under-Secretary-General in the formulation of policies and procedures, as well as in the development of peace-keeping doctrine;

Liaises with all components of the Department in order to coordinate inputs in the development of policies and procedures;

Gathers information on relevant activities undertaken by intergovernmental, regional or non-governmental organizations as well as research institutions;

Analyses and assesses operations and evaluates the results achieved and lessons learned from them;

Prepares reports and studies on issues related to peace-keeping operations as required;

Services the Special Committee on Peace-keeping Operations, that is, prepares pre-session documentation and provides technical and substantive servicing when the Committee is in session;

Provides related services during the sessions of the Special Political and Decolonization Committee (Fourth Committee) of the General Assembly as well as for various other ad hoc intergovernmental committees on issues relating to peace-keeping.

D. Situation Centre 1/

Maintains round-the-clock communications with the field, follows up on events, and collates and disseminates incoming information to those concerned;

Provides daily briefings, analyses of events and statistics on peace-keeping missions;

Follows up on events to amplify and accelerate, in close cooperation with the Office of Operations and with the Office of the Security Coordinator, the information flow from the field;

Provides constant situation displays and monitoring facilities as well as databases, area maps and other reference materials;

Provides information on special situations or topics to the Department and, as required, to the Department of Humanitarian Affairs, the Department of Political Affairs and the Department of Administration and Management;

Serves as a focal point for Member States seeking information on all aspects of peace-keeping matters;

Undertakes urgent action during silent hours with due regard for established procedures.

E. Executive Office

Carries out the standard functions of an executive office as described in the introductory section of the *Manual*;

Administers the Trust Fund for Electoral Assistance.

Appendixes

1. OFFICE OF OPERATIONS

This Office is headed by an Assistant Secretary-General whose general duties and responsibilities are described in the introductory section of the *Manual*.

The main responsibilities of the Office of Operations are as follows:

Is responsible for the day-to-day executive direction of peace-keeping operations and other field missions;

Maintains regular contact with field missions and provides timely direction and guidance on policy issues;

Liaises and coordinates with other departments, especially the Department of Political Affairs and the Department of Humanitarian Affairs, to ensure that guidance to the field is coherent and consistent with established policy and practice;

Maintains contact with the parties to a conflict, with the members of the Security Council, with countries contributing personnel to an operation and with other interested States on matters relating to the efficient discharge of its mandate;

Prepares, in coordination with the Department of Humanitarian Affairs and the Department of Political Affairs, reports of the Secretary-General on peace-keeping operations for the Security Council;

Ensures the efficient implementation and coordination of electoral assistance projects.

The Office comprises four divisions, namely the Africa Division, the Asia and Middle East Division, the Europe and Latin America Division and the Electoral Assistance Division.

(a)   **Africa Division**
(b)   **Asia and Middle East Division**
(c)   **Europe and Latin America Division**

The above-mentioned divisions are organized along regional lines and perform the functions listed under the Office of Operations. Within each Division, responsibility for a peace-keeping operation is assigned to a "desk", comprising one or more political affairs officers, supported by one or more military officers;

(d) Electoral Assistance Division

Advises and assists the Under-Secretary-General, as the focal point for electoral assistance, in handling requests of Member States organizing elections.

2. OFFICE OF PLANNING AND SUPPORT

This Office is headed by an Assistant Secretary-General, whose general duties and responsibilities are described in the introductory section of the *Manual*.

The main functions of the Office of Planning and Support are as follows:

Provides for the overall coordination of all administrative and logistics support activities for field missions, including staffing, finance, logistics and procurement;

Is responsible for the overall planning and coordination of field missions' civilian police, demining and training activities;

Ensures the development and implementation of policies and procedures concerning peace-keeping operations and other field missions;

Initiates, in close cooperation with relevant units of the Office of Operations, initial needs-assessment or fact-finding missions;

Liaises and conducts negotiations with Member States and other organizations regarding contributions to peace-keeping operations and standby arrangements;

Ensures the promulgation of field missions' administrative and financial policies and regulations within the context of United Nations financial and personnel regulations and rules and administrative procedures.

The Office consists of two divisions, namely the Planning Division and the Field Administration and Logistics Division.

(a) Planning Division

Prepares comprehensive operational plans and timetables for new and ongoing peace-keeping operations and other field missions and proposes revisions and modifications of plans as required;

Determines, in cooperation with other units of the Department and, as necessary, with other entities of the United Nations system, the detailed requirements of new peace-keeping operations and other field missions, and examines the implications of changes in the mandates of existing operations in terms of personnel, equipment and cost;

Elaborates and maintains standby arrangements with Governments for the supply of troops, personnel, equipment, financial resources and other services;

Develops guidelines and maintains contact with Governments regarding civilian police serving in field missions;

Coordinates demining activities;

Serves as a focal point for the exchange of information on training for peace-keeping operations and coordinates training activities.

The Division consists of four organizational entities, namely the Mission Planning Service, the Civilian Police Unit, the Demining Unit, and the Training Unit;

(i)　Mission Planning Service

Prepares guidelines (both generic and mission-specific) and procedures according to which the integrated planning for future missions is to be conducted, including directives for inter- and intradepartmental coordination and resource requirements;

Prepares comprehensive operational plans for new peace-keeping operations and other field missions and, as required, revises and modifies plans for current operations and ensures effective implementation;

Prepares the detailed requirements of new peace-keeping operations encompassing timetables, troop contributions, civilian police, personnel and logistics in close cooperation with the Field Administrative and Logistic Division;

Follows up on standby arrangements with Governments for the supply of troops, personnel, equipment, financial resources and other services;

ST/SGB/Organization
Section: DPKO
Page 7
22 March 1995

Analyses operations in progress and completed for lessons learned to assist the Policy and Analysis Unit in the evaluation of results achieved and in the formulation of peace-keeping doctrine;

Maintains an up-to-date database on operations in progress and completed missions, encompassing data on mission conduct, deployment, preparation, finance, personnel, logistics and political developments for all future planning and/or revision of guidelines and procedures;

Develops and maintains an organizational policy for field missions;

(ii) Civilian Police Unit

Provides advice and develops guidelines for the employment, conditions of service, training and administration of civilian police in peace-keeping operations; follows up with permanent missions on agreements with Governments concerning the provision of police for service with the United Nations;

Advises appropriate officers of the Department and field missions on operational police matters;

(iii) Demining Unit

Advises on and plans mine-clearing activities carried out under United Nations auspices; maintains contact with Governments and organizations that participate in these activities or contribute to them;

(iv) Training Unit

Prepares training guidelines, manuals and other relevant training material, in order to assist Member States in preparing their civilian, police and military personnel for peace-keeping operations in a standardized and cost-effective manner;

Encourages Member States to share information and experience on peace-keeping training with the United Nations;

Provides proposals for training of staff participating in peace-keeping operations and assists in the creation of a pool of trained personnel

Appendixes

thoroughly familiar with United Nations rules, regulations and system of operations;

Promotes the training of individuals and units, both civilian and military, engaged in United Nations peace-keeping operations;

(b) Field Administration and Logistics Division

Provides administrative and logistic support to the Organization's peace-keeping and other field missions. In so doing, it supports the substantive activities of the Department of Peace-keeping Operations. It also provides logistic and administrative support to missions undertaken by the Department of Political Affairs, the Department of Humanitarian Affairs and other departments and offices as required (henceforth referred to as "substantive departments");

Identifies, in cooperation with the Mission Planning Service, administrative and logistics requirements of field missions, including administrative support, staffing tables, accommodation, transport, communications, equipment and supplies;

Provides guidance to the chief administrative officers of field missions concerning administrative and logistic policies and procedures, in particular on personnel, finance, communications and procurement matters.

The Division comprises three Services: the Finance Management and Support Service, the Logistics and Communications Service and the Personnel Management and Support Service;

(i) Finance Management Support Service

Provides financial management and support services for field missions from start-up through closure;

Coordinates, prepares and submits to the Controller proposals for resource requirements of field missions for review, finalization and submission to legislative organs;

Reviews and analyses field requirements with a view to ensuring their reasonableness and timely submission to the Controller;

Provides support to substantive departments and field missions to ensure effective resource management and control and provides day-to-day guidance on the application of Financial Regulations and Rules;

Reviews, verifies and certifies claims from Governments for supplies and services, death and disability, as well as for the reimbursement for use of contingent-owned equipment;

Administers financial arrangements in consultation with field missions and Headquarters operational units, including certification of payments for:

- Global vehicle insurance arrangements in conjunction with the Insurance Unit;
- Commercial satellite communications;
- Freight forwarding charges;
- Aircraft operations; and
- Other commercial services;

Administers financial liquidation of existing missions as it pertains to the disposal of equipment, supplies and other assets;

Provides to the Controller reports reflecting overall financial performance, including the financial liquidation of missions and proposals for the redistribution of assets;

Serves as focal point in the Department for compliance with internal control procedures as well as for audit matters relating to field missions;

Makes recommendations for improvements to existing management systems procedures;

Requests revisions to the current financial policy and procedures from the Controller or the Office of Financial Management in the light of their application in field missions;

Provides direct support to the field through the temporary assignment of Finance Officers who act as troubleshooters/advisers, such arrangements being carried out in consultation with the Office of Programme Planning, Budget and Accounts;

Appendixes

(ii) Logistics and Communications Service

In coordination with the Mission Planning Service, develops plans for logistic support for field missions; specifies equipment, supplies and services; assists in determining financial implications;

Produces instructions to carry out those plans and monitors their implementation;

Participates in technical survey teams;

Gathers relevant data to develop logistic support plans for new or expanded missions;

Reassesses periodically the logistics support concepts of field missions and reviews the efficiency of supply arrangements and effectiveness of services provided to the field;

Determines mission start-up requirements and, on the basis of contingency planning activities, assembles, maintains and arranges the deployment of missions' equipment and supplies to permit the rapid initial deployment of key mission elements;

Prepares detailed generic technical and contractual specifications and proposals for the supply of required goods and services;

Determines the method of supply and ensures that the requirements identified are met by raising requisitions for commercial procurement action through the Procurement and Transportation Service or through the issuance of letters of assist for direct supply by Member States;

Determines the need for construction projects, including accommodation facilities, roads and bridges, and renovation and development of military and civilian living and office sites and sanitation facilities in field missions;

Evaluates bids and proposals based on technical criteria, timeliness of delivery and other relevant logistic support aspects;

Manages technical aspects of contracts by establishing appropriate procedures, monitoring the compliance with the terms and conditions of contracts and recommending payment for services received;

Provides technical advice to field missions;

Conducts product research on commonly requisitioned items and market research for logistics supply services;

Manages field mission properties and stock holdings;

Maintains updated records for all field missions;

Monitors expenditures by object of expenditure and their timetable and recommends transfer of allotted funds to the Finance Management Support Service as required to meet priority support demands;

Prepares property survey cases, reviews cases submitted by field missions and submits cases that are supported by the Service to the Headquarters Property Survey Board for consideration and subsequent approval by the Controller;

Determines the need for computer hardware and software and arranges for its supply;

Designs power supply systems, field communications and international systems, making use of satellites, electronic data-processing, radio communications and encryption equipment;

Prepares specifications and evaluates bids and supervises their installation;

Manages movement of contingent personnel and equipment for deployment, rotations and redeployment to field missions;

Prepares specifications for the acquisition of equipment and maintenance of ground and air transport facilities and safety standards;

Investigates and follows up on aircraft accidents and ensures compliance of civilian aircraft operations within United Nations standards;

Appendixes

Assists in the elaboration of guidelines concerning the disposition of United Nations equipment upon the termination of a peace-keeping operation or other field mission and manages their implementation;

(iii) Personnel Management and Support Service

Determines staffing requirements for the civilian component of field missions within the framework of established operational plans;

Administers the Staff Regulations and Rules for field staff and consultants under delegated authority and ensures consistency in the application of personnel policies and practices in the field;

Monitors the various authorities delegated to the field;

Implements and follows up decisions made regarding assignments, separations, promotions, benefits and disciplinary measures of staff in the field;

Serves as the parent department for staff in the Field Service category;

Advises on the selection of senior staff for field assignments;

Identifies personnel resources, including through contractual arrangements;

Makes recommendations to the Office of Human Resources Management on the appointment or assignment of staff to missions and makes arrangements for their briefing, medical clearance and travel;

Evaluates candidates for inclusion on rosters;

Reviews staffing levels in field missions;

Proposes modifications in the categories and numbers of staff as required;

Arranges for travel of military observers, police monitors and Government-provided personnel to the missions in liaison with the permanent missions to the United Nations concerned;

Handles all administrative issues related to their assignment;

Reviews the administrative aspects of the notes for guidance of military observers, civilian police, electoral observers and other Government-provided staff;

Maintains records of field staff and consultants, controls staffing tables and prepares the analytical material necessary to manage staff resources;

Formulates guidelines for the utilization of United Nations Volunteers and contractual personnel; and proposes revisions to personnel policy instruments in the light of their applications in field missions.

Notes

1/   The designation "Centre" as used here is not derived from official organizational nomenclature standards (see General Assembly resolution 32/204; see also A/C.5/33/6).

Appendix D
Department of Peacekeeping Operations: Proposed Budget, 1996-97

Section 3   Peace-keeping operations and special missions

Table 3.1   **Summary of requirements by programme**
(Thousands of United States dollars)

(1) *Regular budget*

Programme	1992-1993 expendi-tures	1994-1995 appropri-ations	Resource growth Amount	Resource growth Percentage	Total before recosting	Recosting	1996-1997 estimates
A. Department of Peace-keeping Operations	10 786.7	12 229.3	3 138.7	25.6	15 368.0	904.6	16 272.6
B. Peace-keeping operations and special missions	63 280.9	71 029.1	(6 299.9)	(8.8)	64 729.2	9 392.3	74 121.5
C. Ad hoc missions	35 201.1	48 963.5	(48 963.5)	(100.0)	—	—	—
Total	**109 268.7**	**132 221.9**	**(52 124.7)**	**(39.4)**	**80 097.2**	**10 296.9**	**90 394.1**

(2) *Extrabudgetary resources*

1992-1993 expendi-tures	1994-1995 estimates	Source of funds	1996-1997 estimates
		(a) Services in support of:	
—	—	(i) United Nations organizations	—
		(ii) Extrabudgetary activities	
13 081.1	36 792.5	Peace-keeping operations	37 963.8
—	—	(b) Substantive activities	—
—	—	(c) Operational projects	—
Total 13 081.1	36 792.5		37 963.8
Total (1) and (2) 122 349.8	169 014.4		128 357.9

Table 3.2   **Summary by object of expenditure**
(Thousands of United States dollars)

(1) *Regular budget*

Object of expenditure	1992-1993 expendi-tures	1994-1995 appropri-ations	Resource growth Amount	Resource growth Percentage	Total before recosting	Recosting	1996-1997 estimates
Posts	71 878.6	77 502.2	(26 947.3)	(34.7)	50 554.9	6 406.9	56 961.8
Other staff costs	12 802.5	14 821.6	(3 330.2)	(22.4)	11 491.4	1 875.9	13 367.3
Consultants and experts	183.1	475.7	(335.1)	(70.4)	140.6	13.6	154.2
Travel	5 672.3	12 912.2	(8 669.4)	(67.1)	4 242.8	349.7	4 592.5
Contractual services	115.4	323.0	(277.4)	(85.8)	45.6	4.1	49.7
General operating expenses	12 144.7	15 078.4	(7 212.3)	(47.8)	7 866.1	1 155.2	9 021.3
Supplies and materials	2 057.1	2 390.6	(400.2)	(16.7)	1 990.4	165.2	2 155.6
Furniture	—	337.9	(337.9)	(100.0)	—	—	—
Equipment	4 414.5	8 051.3	(4 285.9)	(53.2)	3 765.4	326.3	4 091.7
Improvement of premises	—	329.0	(329.0)	(100.0)	—	—	—
Grants and contributions	0.5	—	—	—	—	—	—
Total	**109 268.7**	**132 221.9**	**(52 124.7)**	**(39.4)**	**80 097.2**	**10 296.9**	**90 394.1**

65

(2) Extrabudgetary resources

1992-1993 expendi- tures	1994-1995 estimates	Object of expenditure	1996-1997 estimates
10 811.2	35 387.6	Posts	36 294.0
2 010.8	370.0	Other staff costs	500.0
—	330.0	Travel	160.0
—	704.9	Contractual services	1 009.8
8.2	—	General operating expenses	—
13.2	—	Supplies and materials	—
237.7	—	Equipment	—
Total 13 081.1	36 792.5		37 963.8
Total (1) and (2) 122 349.8	169 014.4		128 357.9

Table 3.3   **Post requirements**

Programme: Peace-keeping operations and special missions

	Established posts		Temporary posts				Total	
	Regular budget		Regular budget		Extrabudgetary resources			
	1994-1995	1996-1997	1994-1995	1996-1997	1994-1995	1996-1997	1994-1995	1996-1997
Professional category and above								
USG	1	1	1	1	—	—	2	2
ASG	3	3	—	—	—	—	3	3
D-2	5	5	—	—	—	—	5	5
D-1	6	8	1	1	8	7	15	16
P-5	7	15	1	1	17	9	25	25
P-4/3	13	14	—	—	84	82	97	96
P-2/1	8	8	—	—	5	5	13	13
Total	43	54	3	3	114	103	160	160
General Service category								
Principal level	1	2	—	—	7	6	8	8
Other levels	22	29	1	1	135	128	158	158
Total	23	31	1	1	142	134	166	166
Other categories								
Local level	190	178	—	—	—	—	190	178
Field Service	180	148	—	—	—	—	180	148
Total	370	326	—	—	—	—	370	326
Grand total	436	411	4	4	256*	237*	696	652

*   Extrabudgetary posts in support of peace-keeping operations include 41 posts proposed for conversion from general temporary assistance (2 D-1, 2 P-5, 8 P-4, 7 P-3 and 22 General Service) and 12 additional posts proposed for 1995 (1 D-1, 4 P-5, 1 P-4 and 6 General Service), and exclude 10 posts transferred to the Office of Programme Planning, Budget and Accounts effective 14 February 1995 (1 P-4, 3 P-3, 1 P-2 and 5 General Service).

Source: United Nations

Appendix E
Cost of Peacekeeping Operations

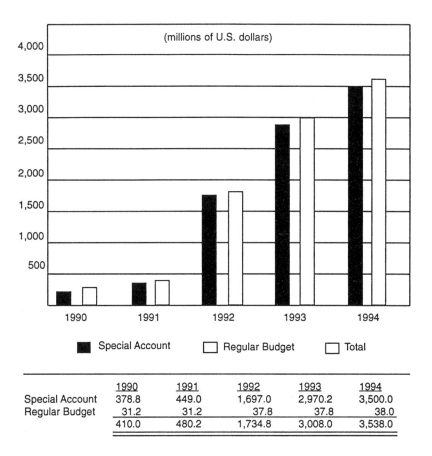

(millions of U.S. dollars)

Special Account   Regular Budget   Total

	1990	1991	1992	1993	1994
Special Account	378.8	449.0	1,697.0	2,970.2	3,500.0
Regular Budget	31.2	31.2	37.8	37.8	38.0
	410.0	480.2	1,734.8	3,008.0	3,538.0

UNITED NATIONS FIELD OPERATIONS
Growth of Total Field Mission Budgets 1990-1994

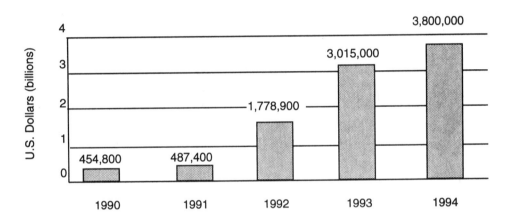

Percentage growth by year:	90-91	91-92	92-93	93-94*
	7%	265%	69%	26%

* 1994 figures are estimates
all figures at year end

Appendix F
Department of Humanitarian Affairs: Strategic Plan

I. INTRODUCTION

The Department of Humanitarian Affairs was established pursuant to General Assembly Resolution 46/182, under the leadership of the Emergency Relief Coordinator and Under-Secretary-General for Humanitarian Affairs. Its principal purpose is to ensure the timely, coherent and coordinated response of the international Community to disasters and emergencies. This includes the promotion of prevention, preparedness and mitigation measures aimed at the reduction of vulnerability of those affected by such events. The Department is also responsible for facilitating the smooth transition from emergency relief to rehabilitation and development.

In 1994 the Under-Secretary-General completed a process of restructuring the Department aimed at achieving clarity in the respective functions of its New York and Geneva offices and a more effective utilization of its resources. This is followed by the preparation of a strategic plan in 1995 to define the objectives and priorities of the Department as a whole in order to bring greater focus to its activities. He further decided that this would be followed by a management study to identify the core resources needed for the implementation of the Strategy Plan and in that context, measures to further improve the efficiency of the Department.

This document sets out the Department's objectives and priorities. It has been produced on the basis of extensive consultation with the staff both at Headquarters and in the field. It also draws on the views expressed by Governments, humanitarian agencies, other entities within the UN system and NGOs.

II. MISSION STATEMENT

The mission of the UN Department of Humanitarian Affairs, led by the Emergency Relief Coordinator, is to mobilize and coordinate the collective efforts of the international community, in particular those of the UN System, to meet the needs of those exposed to human suffering and material destruction in disasters and emergencies in a coherent and timely manner. It also includes the reduction of vulnerability, the promotion of solutions to root causes and the facilitation of the smooth transition from relief to rehabilitation and development.

III. FRAMEWORK

In order to fulfil its mission, DHA will focus on achieving objectives and priorities in the following areas, working closely with members of IASC, governments and other partners:

1. The establishment of humanitarian policy.

2. The advocacy of humanitarian principles and concerns.

3. The coordination of humanitarian actions.

4. The strengthening of capacity at the local, national and international levels.

5. The collection, analysis and dissemination of information.

6. The mobilization of resources.

IV. STRATEGIC OBJECTIVES

1. **The Establishment of Humanitarian Policy**

A clear vision for collective and effective action by the humanitarian community is central to the task of improving the consistency and coherence of humanitarian operations. General principles governing humanitarian action and their relationship with Human Rights principles must be clearly established and agreed upon. From those principles, practical policies need to be developed, both in response to disasters and emergencies and in efforts to reduce the vulnerability of those at risk.

DHA's strategic objectives in this area therefore are:

(i)   To facilitate the refinement of international norms for humanitarian action, with particular emphasis on the critical need for ensuring humanitarian space and access to those in need in conflict situations and to integrate these norms into a set of principles governing humanitarian assistance.

(ii)   To define, based on the principles mentioned above, a set of consistent policies adapted for each emergency or disaster, including recommendations for preventive action.

(iii)   To promote the establishment of policies for the integration of prevention, preparedness and mitigation measures into national planning processes.

In pursuit of these objectives DHA will, <u>inter alia</u>:

-   Support the further refinement of humanitarian principles and the development of humanitarian policies through detailed evaluations of particular humanitarian operations.

-   Strengthen its capacity to play a leading role in shaping the international response to impending emergencies.

-   Continue to contribute to efforts to define better the respective roles and responsibilities of humanitarian, political and military actors in emergencies both in the field and at headquarters.

-   Elaborate a policy framework for improving linkages between relief action and the development process, including principles governing the transfer of responsibilities for coordination from relief to rehabilitation and development.

2. The Advocacy of Humanitarian Principles and Concerns

The ERC has a specific responsibility to be an advocate for humanitarian principles and concerns. The ERC will bring these issues to the attention of both those entrusted with humanitarian work and others whose decisions may influence such action.

DHA's strategic objectives in this area therefore are:

(i)   To advocate recognition of humanitarian principles and policies and to ensure their respect by all concerned.

(ii)   To identify and bring to the attention of the international community those instances when these principles have been violated, and to initiate actions to remedy the situation.

(iii)   To promote the creation of a public constituency for humanitarian work and to galvanize its support for increased resources for humanitarian operations.

(iv)   To ensure that the humanitarian dimension is fully reflected in the planning and implementation of the overall UN response to crisis situations.

(v)   To raise awareness of the need for effective prevention, preparedness and response to disasters and emergencies.

In pursuit of these objectives the DHA will, inter alia,:

- Develop, on the basis of the observation and analysis of current practice, a strategy for mobilizing support for the mitigation of the effects of disasters and emergencies and for investment in prevention and preparedness.

- Develop, on the basis of an understanding of the comparative advantages a strategy for raising awareness of humanitarian principles and policies in which the advocacy of different actors is undertaken in the most effective manner.

- Elaborate on a set of model frameworks and agreements which could be used for negotiations with conflicting parties on securing humanitarian access to affected people.

- Set out a process for the more systematic use of early warning information to ensure that this results in practical recommendations for decision-making.

3.   **The Coordination of humanitarian actions**

The ERC's responsibility in promoting a culture of cooperation within a multi-mandate system, drawing on the comparative strength of each actor, requires him to ensure the most effective use of scarce resources for the benefit of those in need.

DHA's strategic objectives in this area therefore are:

(i)   To formulate, in collaboration with all relevant actors, a strategy for each disaster or emergency, based on comprehensive and prioritised humanitarian assistance requirements;

(ii)   To allocate responsibilities among the humanitarian organizations of the UN system;

(iii)   To develop consistent approaches to the co-ordination of prevention, preparedness and mitigation activities at national and international levels.

In pursuit of these objectives the DHA will, inter alia,:

- Produce standard guidelines for assessment, and training programmes for staff including at field level, in relevant operational techniques.

- Develop a structure within DHA allowing the Department more efficiently to lead and support interagency missions and assessment teams.

- Seek improvements in emergency rules and regulations to ensure the speedy processing of administrative, procurement and recruitment questions, the rapid deployment of coordinating teams, and effective administrative support for field operations.

- Put in place an effective capacity for support to in-country coordination, to include:

    - greater clarity on the role of the Humanitarian Coordinator and his/her relationship with other UN actors in the field, including the Resident Co-ordinator, where this is a separate function;

    - promoting an interagency agreement on the special role and activities of DHA at field level;

    - a comprehensive set of systems and procedures for technical and logistical support.

4. The Strengthening of Capacity at Local, National and International Levels

The ERC's role in leading international efforts to reduce vulnerability and improve emergency response begins with supporting efforts to improve the capacity of local, national and international actors in prevention, preparedness and mitigation, as well as in response.

DHA's strategic objectives in this area therefore are:

(i) To strengthen national capacity for the reduction of vulnerability through the integration of effective measures into national planning processes.

(ii) To develop appropriate recommendations for improvements in local, national and international capacity drawing on the experience of humanitarian operations.

In pursuit of these objectives DHA will, inter alia,:

- Support the further strengthening of technical assistance available to disaster-prone countries.

- Co-ordinate and, where appropriate, develop systems for national and international emergency standby capacities, including human resources, to ensure the most beneficial use of these tools by humanitarian actors.

- Work with humanitarian partners to identify key policy and operational issues as a basis for the setting of criteria for the selection of cases for evaluation.

Establish a modus operandi with Governments, humanitarian agencies and other Departments within the UN Secretariat for the design and implementation of evaluation studies as well as for the application of the recommendations which thereby result.

5. **The collection, analysis and dissemination of information**

Information and its timely analysis and dissemination is a prerequisite for effective prevention, preparedness, mitigation and response to disasters and emergencies. It provides a sound basis for policy and advocacy and thus of decision making.

DHA's strategic objectives in this area therefore are:

(i)   To ensure that appropriate information is available for timely analysis as a basis for effective decisions.

(ii)   To ensure that relevant information is available both to the ERC and the international community to assist in the development of policy and the advocacy of principles.

In pursuit of these objectives the DHA will, inter alia,:

-       Put in place an effective emergency information system for reduction of risk, early warning, preventive action and timely, consistent and proactive response.

-       Strengthen arrangements for the collection, analysis and dissemination of information relevant to field operations, including the tracking of financial requirements, donors' contributions and resource utilization.

6. **The Mobilisation of Resources**

None of the objectives identified above can be realised without the proper mobilizing and allocation of resources.

DHA's strategic objectives in this area therefore are:

(i)   To organize and lead joint efforts, where required, for the mobilization of sufficient resources to meet priority needs, both of those affected and of Governments involved in prevention, preparedness, mitigation and early recovery activities.

(ii)   To improve processes for the management and early use of voluntary Trust Funds.

In pursuit of these objectives the DHA will, inter alia,:

-       Devise a means for mobilising immediate resources for field coordination.

-       Ensure that a resource mobilisation plan is integrated into the Consolidated Appeal Process.

-       Support strategies for the mobilisation of resources for immediate recovery and rehabilitation activities.

-       Assist and promote international and national efforts to mobilise resources for prevention, preparedness and mitigation.

-       On the basis of the identification of core functions of the Department, draw up a Financial Strategy to provide for the long-term financial viability of DHA.

V. CONCLUSIONS

DHA will formulate work plans to implement the above mentioned strategic objectives and priorities. The first of which will be for the biennium 1996 - 1997. The strategic objectives and priorities, as well as the work plan, will be reviewed in light of future development.

The strategic objectives set out above present a formidable challenge. Their successful realization will depend upon the understanding and support of humanitarian and other concerned partners.

In addition, there are two resources which are necessary prerequisites for success: a sound financial base for the Department, and an effective and unified staff.

To this end, a management study will be commissioned to identify core staff resources required to realize the strategic objectives of the Department as well as to recommend measures to improve its efficiency. A financial strategy will then be formulated to mobilize the necessary financial resources to put the Department on a viable and sustainable basis.

Appendix G
Department of Humanitarian Affairs:
Proposed Budget 1996-97

Section 24   Department of Humanitarian Affairs :

Table 24.1   **Summary of requirements by programme**
(Thousands of United States dollars)

(1) *Regular budget*

Programme		1992-1993 expendi- tures	1994-1995 appropri- ations	Resource growth Amount	Resource growth Percentage	Total before recosting	Recosting	1996-1997 estimates
A.	Executive direction and management	2 614.3	2 907.0	45.6	1.5	2 952.6	165.9	3 118.5
B.	Programme of work	11 078.8	12 368.2	248.5	2.0	12 616.7	543.2	13 159.9
C.	Programme support	1 249.0	3 759.5	55.8	1.4	3 815.3	206.5	4 021.8
	Total	14 942.1	19 034.7	349.9	1.8	19 384.6	915.6	20 300.2

(2) *Extrabudgetary resources*

1992-1993 expendi- tures	1994-1995 estimates	Source of funds	1996-1997 estimates
		(a) Services in support of:	
—	—	(i) United Nations organizations	—
		(ii) Extrabudgetary activities	
		Special Account for Programme	
		Support Costs of the Department	
2 840.0	5 022.0	of Humanitarian Affairs	5 528.6
		(b) Substantive activities	
2 980.2	1 340.6	African Emergency Trust Fund	1 060.0
6 460.3	4 543.0	Afghanistan Emergency Trust Fund	4 489.0
		Emergency Trust Fund for	
13 191.0	5 762.4	Humanitarian Assistance for Iraq	5 099.8
33 931.8	2 125.4	Kampuchean Emergency Trust Fund	ɀ/
		Sasakawa Disaster Prevention Award	
124.7	150.0	Endowment Fund	160.0
		Trust Fund for the United Nations	
51 582.4	28 497.8	Guard Contingent in Iraq	19 800.0
375.0	500.0	Trust Fund for Chernobyl	150.0
82 807.6	60 138.0	Trust Fund for Disaster Relief Assistance	60 138.0
		Trust Fund for the International Decade	
2 145.8	3 469.8	for Natural Disaster Reduction	1 732.4
		Trust Fund for Repatriation of	
2 297.9	129.4	Cambodian Refugees	ɀ/
—	6 000.0	Trust Fund for Rwanda	—
		Trust Fund for Strengthening the Office	
3 046.7	3 613.0	of the Emergency Relief Coordinator	5 045.4
		Voluntary Trust Fund for Assistance in	
—	4 994.6	Mine Clearance	10 470.3
		(c) Operational projects	
45 167.6	26 457.0	Afghanistan Emergency Trust Fund	25 511.0
		Trust Fund for Technical Cooperation	
2 523.0	5 420.0	Activities	5 500.0
Total 249 474.0	158 163.0		144 684.5
Total (1) and (2) 264 416.1	177 197.7		164 984.7

ɀ/   No information is currently available on projected expenditure in 1996-1997.

Source: UN document A/50/6 (Section 24) 21 April 1995

Appendix H
DPKO Situation Centre

UNITED NATIONS
DEPARTMENT OF PEACE-KEEPING OPERATIONS (DPKO)
SITUATION CENTRE

1. The Situation Centre was formed in April 1993 in the Department of Peace-Keeping Operations, to provide situation monitoring and exchange of information services between the headquarters in New York and UN field missions worldwide. The mandate has been described as follows:

    > "The Situation Room is intended to speed up, complement and amplify the information flows generated in the field to facilitate timely decisions by the Under-Secretary-General for Peace-Keeping Operations. Its role is to maintain communications links with all missions, to solicit information from the field as well as to process and analyze raw incoming information....
    > Its staff, organized in teams to provide coverage around the clock, will screen incoming information, respond immediately to factual queries, judge when to contact senior decision makers and to summarize incoming information...
    > [In the final stage] the Situation Room will also be in a position to provide daily briefings to senior managers, present spontaneous briefings upon request, maintain constant situation displays and continuous event monitoring and display..... with reference to relevant information using maps, statistics and basic political, military and economic information as well as access to in-house and public data bases."

2. Furthermore, the Secretary General stated in August 1993 that:

    > "arrangements will be made, through the Situation Room now being established by DPKO, to ensure that security staff can be reached at all times."

3. The Situation Room was renamed the Situation Centre and is located on the 32nd floor of the main Secretariat building. The address is:
    UNITED NATIONS, DEPARTMENT OF PEACE-KEEPING OPERATIONS,
    SITUATION CENTRE, S-3260, NEW YORK, NY 10017, USA

4. Tasks of the Situation Centre include the following:

    - Provide 24-hour point of contact
    - Maintain uninterrupted communications with ALL UN peace-keeping missions and be able to communicate with all other UN-missions around the globe;
    - Solicit information from the field;
    - Collate and disseminate timely raw information;
    - Develop, in coordination with UN headquarters services, enhanced communications, data processing and multiple visual display facilities;
    - Prepare consolidated summaries;
    - Provide daily briefings to senior managers and spontaneous briefings upon request;
    - Maintain constant situation displays and provide continuous event monitoring;

- Provide reference materials (including maps, statistics and basic political military and economic analytical information) via access to in-house and public data bases;
- Develop an in-house capability to amplify and synthesize the information flow from the field;
- Monitor developing regional situations around the world, that could affect the general security and safety of UN personnel, using all available news media and UN information channels;
- Provide a Crisis Centre in the event that a peace-keeping mission has to be implemented on a short notice, or a crisis occurs in one of the established missions or elsewhere.

5.   In order to meet these requirements and to respond efficiently to the needs generated by the above described functions, the SITCEN is organized as follows:

- **Management Team** including the chief, deputy chief and office management,
- **Duty Room** operating 24 hours-a-day, staffed by 12 to 15 officers, a supervisor and a communications specialist,
- **Information and Research** function staffed by four officers and one research assistant, responsible for maintaining and expanding data and background information required for situation reports or briefings, and
- **Automation Support** function staffed by one officer and a technical specialist, responsible for the development and maintenance of the technical support system and training of staff.

The staff currently comprises 28 personnel, 9 civilians and 19 military. At this time, all of the military except five are provided by member states on a no-cost to the UN basis. On the average, about 20 countries are represented in the SITCEN staff. The objective over time is to recruit more civilian staff and to place more of the military staff on contract to the United Nations.

Updated 20/11/95

INFORMATION AND RESEARCH UNIT
SITUATION CENTRE

PURPOSE:
- TO RESEARCH REQUESTS FOR INFORMATION FROM PEACE-KEEPING MISSIONS AND ELEMENTS OF DPKO AT SECRETARIAT LEVEL
  -- ALSO SUPPORT REQUESTS FROM OTHER PARTS OF SECRETARIAT, UN AGENCIES (I.E., SECGEN, DPA, DHA, UNICEF, ETC)

- TO PROVIDE A POINT OF CONTACT FOR RECEIPT AND DISSEMINATION WITHIN DPKO OF SENSITIVE / RESTRICTED INFORMATION FROM MEMBER STATES
  -- INFORMATION DISSEMINATED TO OTHER SECRETARIAT DEPARTMENTS / UN AGENCIES WITH NEED TO KNOW AND IF INFORMATION MEETS REQUIREMENTS

- TO REGULARLY UPDATE THE DPKO LEADERSHIP THROUGH WRITTEN PRODUCTS AND BRIEFINGS ON SIGNIFICANT DEVELOPMENTS THAT MAY AFFECT PEACE-KEEPING OPERATIONS NOW AND IN THE FUTURE
  -- "FUTURE" IS PART OF EARLY WARNING PROCESS

RESOURCES:
- FIVE PERSONNEL: THREE MILITARY OFFICERS, ONE CIVILIAN, ONE SENIOR NCO
- INTERNAL UN REPORTING (FIELD, HEADQUARTERS, UN AGENCIES)
- MEDIA
- COMPANIES SUCH AS OXFORD ANALYTICA, ECONOMIST INTELLIGENCE UNIT
- CONTROL RISKS (COMPANY THAT PRODUCES THREAT ASSESSMENTS FOR BUSINESS COMMUNITY)
- INTERNET
- MEMBER STATES' INFORMATION

Appendix I
Central Emergency Revolving Fund

CONSOLIDATED ADVANCES AND REIMBURSEMENTS
(As of 29 September 1995)

OPERATIONAL ORGANIZATION	PROJECT	AMOUNT ADVANCED	AMOUNT REIMBURSED	AMOUNT OUTSTANDING	DATE OF ADVANCE	DATE OF REIMBURSEMENT
UNICEF	KENYA	2,000,000	2,000,000	0	24/08/92	31/12/92 & 22/10/93
UNICEF	SOMALIA	5,000,000	5,000,000	0	24/08/92	22/12/92
UNCHS	SOMALIA	500,000	500,000	0	10/09/92	29/01/93
FAO	SOMALIA	1,600,000	1,600,000	0	30/09/92	24/06/93
WHO	SOMALIA	2,000,000	2,000,000	0	26/10/92	29/03/93
UNICEF	IRAQ	5,000,000	5,000,000	0	11/11/92	15/04/93
UNHCR	AFGHANISTAN	5,000,000	5,000,000	0	24/11/92	06/01/93
UNICEF	MOZAMBIQUE	2,000,000	2,000,000	0	22/01/93	02/02/94 & 01/08/94
WFP	TAJIKISTAN	4,500,000	2,036,121	2,463,879	25/03/93	03/05/94 & 10/06/94
WHO	YUGOSLAVIA	2,500,000	2,500,000	0	26/03/93	05/05/94
UNHCR	GEORGIA	2,000,000	2,000,000	0	22/04/93	16/09/93
UNICEF	IRAQ	5,000,000	5,000,000	0	14/06/93	21/10/93
UNHCR	TAJIKISTAN	5,000,000	5,000,000	0	18/06/93	29/12/93 & 05/94
WFP	IRAQ	4,000,000	4,000,000	0	21/06/93	03/05/94 & 09/08/94
UNICEF	HAITI	1,000,000	1,000,000	0	23/07/93	25/04/94 & 01/08/94
WFP	LEBANON	560,000	560,000	0	03/09/93	03/01/94 (FAO)
UNCHS	LEBANON	5,000,000	1,693,276	3,306,724	09/09/93	21/03/94 & 17/06/94
UNICEF	IRAQ	7,000,000	7,000,000	0	27/10/93	01/02/94
UNHCR	BURUNDI	5,000,000	5,000,000	0	19/11/93	01/06/94
WFP	BURUNDI	5,000,000	5,000,000	0	22/12/93	03/05/94
UNICEF	ANGOLA	1,500,000	1,500,000	0	06/01/94	19/05/94
IOM	ZAIRE	1,000,000	649,846	350,154	06/01/94	08/07/94
UNICEF	SUDAN	1,000,000	1,000,000	0	17/02/94	20/06/94
FAO	SUDAN	200,000	200,000	0	23/02/94	16/05/94
UNICEF	YUGOSLAVIA	1,000,000	1,000,000	0	16/03/94	31/08/94
UNDP	KENYA	500,000	500,000	0	18/03/94	13/04/95
WHO	YUGOSLAVIA	2,500,000	2,500,000	0	29/03/94	31/10/94
UNICEF	SOMALIA	4,870,000	4,870,000	0	28/04/94	22/07/94 & 24/10/94
UNREO	RWANDA	200,000	200,000	0	28/04/94	08/09/94
UNHCR	TAJIKISTAN	3,000,000	3,000,000	0	20/05/94	21/12/94
UNHCR	RWANDA	10,000,000	10,000,000	0	01/06/94	29/09/94 & 21/11/94
UNICEF	RWANDA	3,000,000	3,000,000	0	21/07/94	30/12/94
WFP	RWANDA	5,000,000	5,000,000	0	22/07/94	17/11/94

Complex Emergencies

HCHR/HR	RWANDA	3,000,000	0	3,000,000	07/10/94	
UNICEF	SUDAN	3,000,000	1,684,721	1,315,279	28/12/94	24/05/95
UNICEF	N. IRAQ	930,000	930,000	0	04/01/95	26/04/95
UCAH	ANGOLA	480,600	480,600	0	27/01/95	29/06/95 & 6/09/95
WFP	RWANDA	5,000,000	5,000,000	0	07/03/95	07/07/95
UNREO	RWANDA	100,000	0	100,000	11/07/95	
UNREO	RWANDA	100,000	0	100,000	01/08/95	
SRSG	BURUNDI	110,000	0	110,000	28/08/95	
UNREO	RWANDA	200,000	0	200,000		
UNAMIR	RWANDA	2,000,000	0	2,000,000		
		118,350,600	105,404,564	12,946,036		

Status of Utilization of the Fund:

Contributions received: $49,218,252

Less: Advances   (118,350,600)
Add: Reimbursements   105,404,564
Add: Interest Earned (as of 31 Aug. 95)   3,294,169

Fund Balance as of 29 September 1995 $ 39,566,385

(DHA 29 September 1995)

Appendixes

	Pledges	Collections	Date Paid
Algeria	20,000	20,000	07 Dec 94
Australia	800,000	743,600	27 Jul 92
Austria	500,000	500,000	30 Mar 92
Belgium	330,000	327,327	17 Sep 92
Canada	2,300,000	2,195,321	16 & 22 Jun 92
Colombia	10,000	10,000	4 Feb 93
Denmark	2,000,000	1,999,985	31 Aug 92
Finland	1,500,000	1,533,804	18 Jun 92
France	5,600,000	934,579	16 Nov 92
		4,545,455	8 & 27 Jan 93
Germany	5,000,000	5,000,000	30 Jun 92
Holy See	50,000	50,000	22 May 92
	20,000	20,000	& 20 Dec 94
Iceland	10,000	10,000	6 Jul 92
Ireland	100,000	100,000	18 Jun 92
Italy	5,000,000	4,284,184	10 Dec 92
Japan	5,000,000	5,000,000	27 Jul 92
Korea, Republic of	50,000	50,000	11 Jun 92
Libyan Arab Jamahiriya	5,000	5,000	6 Oct 93
Liechtenstein	7,000	6,641	10 Apr 92
Luxembourg	100,000	100,000	13 Aug 92
Malaysia	20,000	20,000	15 Jun 93
Mauritius	10,000	10,000	1 Jul 92
Monaco	40,111.73	20,000	19 Jul 94
		22,260	& 4 May 1995
Netherlands	3,000,000	3,083,590	12 Jun 92
New Zealand	140,000	136,825	23 Mar 92
Norway	1,850,000	1,849,970	5 May & 10 Jun 92
Philippines	20,000	20,000	19 Sept 95
Russian Federation		250,000	23 May 95
Spain	750,000	671,544	7 Jun 93
		88,453	4 Mar 94
Sweden	2,750,000	2,408,744	25 Nov 92
Switzerland	2,000,000	999,985	25 Aug 92
		999,985	& 13 Jan 93
United Kingdom	5,000,000	5,000,000	24 Apr 92
United States	6,200,000	2,500,000	15 Apr 92
		3,700,000	23 Feb & 19 Jul 93
NGOs	1,000	1,000	17 Jun 92
Total Contributions	**$ 50,183,111**	**$ 49,218,252**	

Appendix J
Note on DHA/DPKO/DPA Cooperation

DRAFT   21 November 1994

Background

1.   In its resolution 46/120 of 18 December 1992 on "Agenda for Peace" the General Assembly encouraged the Secretary-General "to address the question of coordination, when necessary, between humanitarian assistance programs and peace-keeping or related operations, preserving the non-political, neutral and impartial character of humanitarian action".

2. In his report to the General Assembly on the work of the Organization (A/48/1), the Secretary-General noted:

> "The international community has asked that more be done to strengthen the capacity of the United Nations to provide humanitarian assistance, through coordinated planning and implementation involving the Departments of Political Affairs, Peace-keeping Operations and Humanitarian Affairs, and that humanitarian concerns should be reflected in fact-finding missions and in peace-keeping operations. I have therefore taken steps to insure that essential collaboration takes place among those Departments and between them and all other United Nations organizations and bodies. I stress again that it is essential that the United Nations should develop the ability to link humanitarian action and protection of human rights with peacemaking, peace-keeping and peace-building."

3.   The General Assembly in its resolution 48/42 of 10 December 1993 on peace-keeping operations, suggested that, "the emergency relief coordinator should be fully consulted in the overall planning of a peace-keeping operation when the mandate for such an operation contains a humanitarian component and in other cases should be consulted at an early stage when close coordination between humanitarian and peace-keeping activities is required".

4.   In its resolution 48/57 of 14 December 1993 the General Assembly stressed the importance of the full participation of the Emergency Relief Coordinator "in the overall United Nations planning of responses to emergencies in order to serve as the humanitarian advocate in ensuring that the humanitarian dimension, particularly the principles of humanity, neutrality and impartiality of humanitarian assistance is taken fully into account."

5. Additionally, in the Secretary-General's Statement to the Informal Working Group on "An Agenda for Peace", 21 May 1993 he stated, "Humanitarian assistance is closely connected with preventive diplomacy, early warning and the maintenance of international peace and security. It is associated with fact-finding, the prevention of conflicts and emergencies, and with peacemaking, peace-keeping and peacebuilding."

6. It is in this spirit that DPA, DPKO and DHA have engaged in a discussion on the integration of elements of the analysis, planning and implementation of the three Departments.

7. What follows developed as a result of this dialogue and is intended as a framework for interaction among planning and desk officers of the three Departments, for early warning analysis and operational planning in situations of common interest. This staff-level interaction should complement and provide support for the regular meetings at the USG and director level held among the three Departments. The experience obtained working on the next two-three complex, conflict related emergencies, should reveal forms of interaction that prove to be useful, and those that require further changes.

Framework for Cooperation

8. Desk and planning officers from the three Departments will interact continuously with each other in monitoring early warning signals and participating in joint analysis and consultative meetings as appropriate, in the planning of preventive action, and humanitarian and peace-keeping operations in the field.

9. The three Departments will interact, primarily through their desk officers, in the following ways:

- exchanges of information such as early warning signals, staff reports, internal meeting notes, maps, assessments, agency sit reps, etc.;

- staff consultations to review and interpret a developing situation;

- informal inputs into the planning of the other two Department's operations;

- contributions towards the drafting of reports and for the preparation of plans of the other Department;

- DPKO and DPA will participate in the briefing of humanitarian coordinators and DHA will participate in the briefing of Force Commanders;

- DPKO and DHA will participate in briefing the special envoy or special representative when appointed.

10. DHA, DPKO and DPA have "integrated" their planning/operations monitoring flow charts, which now indicate the level and content of the staff interaction expected. Information briefings will familiarize planning and desk officers with this framework for cooperation.

11. A copy of the flow chart is attached. It should however be understood that the chart is not intended to imply a uniform symmetry in time among the planning and monitoring activities of the three Departments. Each complex emergency will present different circumstances and be handled in a different fashion. Not all of the action points will occur in the planning of every operation. That said, following are some of the action points that should involve interaction between the respective staffs.

Cooperation in the Planning Phase

12. In the context of pre-crisis consultations, it will be important for all three Departments to be looking at the same problem (albeit through different lenses). The three Departments will share country profiles, risk maps, information on indicators, early warning signals, and information from the field, including monitoring reports and other reports from the Resident Coordinator and other UN and NGO sources. Routine monitoring of country situations will be maintained through regular information sharing by UN organizations and agencies at the country level. All situation reports regularly provided by the Resident Coordinator to the Office of the Administrator will be promptly routed to DPA, DHA, and DPKO and other relevant UN Departments. Information will also be drawn from outside published sources, member state information, and from a variety of early warning data bases accessed through Internet. This information will be jointly analyzed to permit common, or at least compatible, interpretations.

13. If there are initial field missions (usually conducted by humanitarian agency field staff) to determine the dimensions of the crisis, the results will be shared and jointly reviewed. In consultation, the planning/desk officers will undertake a preliminary survey of military, logistical and humanitarian "assets", personnel and material, related to the event or events, with direct input from UN agencies, international organizations and non-governmental-organizations. (Example: WFP, UNHCR or FALD data on local storage or port off-take capacity, or fuel sources and prices.) Lacunae will be pinpointed. The Departments will undertake to arrive at common, or compatible, assessments of the situation.

14. The Departments will keep each other fully informed while planning the initial surveys/assessments, and where appropriate, possibilities will be explored for joint undertakings in terms of cross participation. The objective will be survey/assessment reports with compatible information and conclusions. These reports will be shared with relevant UN agencies and appropriate organizations.

15. DHA, and through DHA, UN agencies, international organizations and non-governmental organizations, will contribute, as appropriate, to the conduct of the DPKO technical survey, the drafting of the DPKO operational concept and the mission support concept, and will have the opportunity to review and comment upon the draft Status of Forces Agreement (SOFA) and the initial cost analysis.

16. With a view to ensuring compatible humanitarian and peace-keeping operations DHA will, as appropriate, provide inputs on the humanitarian dimensions of the crisis, in preparation of the DPKO operations plan. DPKO and DHA will provide input to DPA for the drafting of the reports of the Secretary-General for the Security Council.

17. Conversely, DPKO and DPA will be invited, as necessary, to contribute to relevant reports for intergovernmental bodies and for the elaboration of a humanitarian strategy for addressing complex emergencies. DHA will share with DPKO and DPA the Inter-Agency Consolidated Appeals for Humanitarian Assistance prepared under its leadership with relevant UN agencies and other organizations.

18. When demobilization, demining and other common activities, are part of the UN operation, DHA and DPKO will integrate their planning processes.

Cooperation in the Operations Phase

19. Desk officers from the three Departments will continue to exchange information and to liaise as necessary throughout the operations phase, to the reduction and eventual closing down of the peace-keeping operations. As required, interdepartmental working groups will be formed to effect this coordination/cooperation.

20. The DPKO Situation Centre will be available as a 24 hour information link between DHA New York and humanitarian coordinators in the field. In times of crisis involving significant new humanitarian impacts on civilian populations, or potential risk to humanitarian assistance personnel in the field, DHA will staff one of the work stations in the situation centre briefing room to provide open channels to the humanitarian community.

21. Coordination between humanitarian organizations and UN military operations in the field will be effected through the aegis of the office of the Humanitarian Coordinator, or directly as the exigencies of the situation require. In the event that circumstances in the field necessitate a reformulation of the peace-keeping mission, many if not most of the above steps would be repeated, with the same or similar info sharing cooperation/joint activities.

22. The obvious benefit to be derived from routinized DHA/DPKO/DPA interaction in planning of UN military missions is the opportunity to ensure that the size, composition, deployment and rules of engagement of the force are elaborated with the needs of the humanitarian assistance operations and the realities of the political situation in mind, particularly in those situations where protection of assistance activities is part of the mission's mandate.

23. While the importance of horizontal coordination has frequently been emphasized by member states, it should be understood that the "integrated" planning process is in no way to erode the neutrality and impartiality of humanitarian assistance operations. Indeed, it is expected that through this enhanced consultative process humanitarian concerns will be more forcefully reflected in UN operations and that humanitarian mandates will be more effectively protected.

DHA, New York

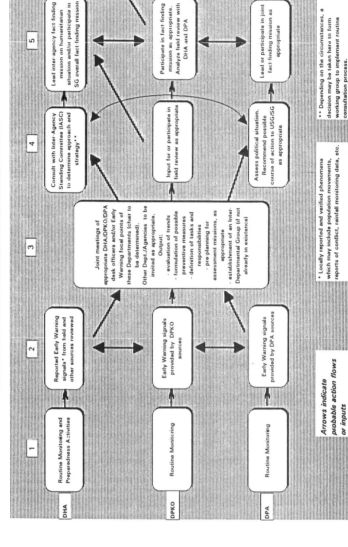

DRAFT

COORDINATION OF DHA, DPKO AND DPA ACTIVITIES
IN PLANNING AND IMPLEMENTING COMPLEX OPERATIONS IN THE FIELD

6 January 1995

DHA

1	2	3	4	5

Routine Monitoring and Preparedness Activities → Reported Early Warning signals* from field and other sources reviewed

Joint meetings of appropriate DHA/DPKO/DPA desk officers and/or Early Warning focal points of these Departments (chair to be determined). Other Dept./Agencies to be invited as appropriate.
Output:
- evaluation of trends
- formulation of possible preventive measures
- definition of tasks and responsibilities
- pre-planning for assessment missions, as appropriate
- establishment of an Inter-Departmental Group (if not already in existence)

Consult with Inter-Agency Standing Committee (IASC) to determine approach and strategy**

Lead inter-agency fact finding mission on humanitarian situation and/or participate in SG overall fact finding mission

DPKO

Routine Monitoring → Early Warning signals provided by DPKO sources

Input for or participate in field review as appropriate

Participate in fact finding mission as appropriate. Analyze field review with DHA and DPA

DPA

Routine Monitoring → Early Warning signals provided by DPA sources

Assess political situation. Recommend possible course of action to USG/SG as appropriate

Lead or participate in joint fact finding mission as appropriate

Arrows indicate probable action flows or inputs

* Locally reported and verified phenomena which may include population movements, reports of conflict, rainfall monitoring data, etc.

** Depending on the circumstances, a decision may be taken here to form working group to implement routine consultation process.

N.B. While arrows indicate that interaction occurs between activities, the flow is not intended to convey absolute symmetry. Any Department may be in a different position in time or sequence, depending on the situation.

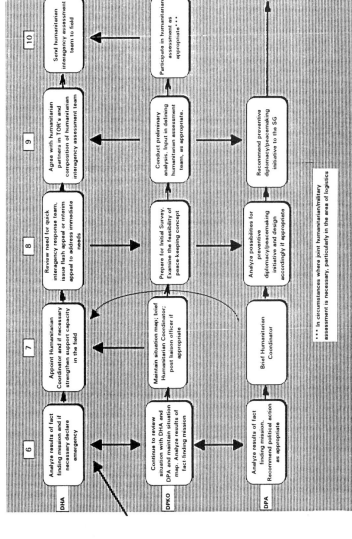

DRAFT

COORDINATION OF DHA, DPKO AND DPA ACTIVITIES
IN PLANNING AND IMPLEMENTING COMPLEX OPERATIONS IN THE FIELD

6 January 1995

DHA

| 6 | 7 | 8 | 9 | 10 |

Analyze results of fact finding mission and if necessary declare emergency

Appoint Humanitarian Coordinator and if necessary strengthen support capacity in the field

Review need for quick interagency response team, issue flash appeal or interim appeal to address immediate needs

Agree with humanitarian partners in TOR's and composition of humanitarian interagency assessment team

Send humanitarian interagency assessment team to field

DPKO

Continue to review situation with DHA and DPA and maintain situation map. Analyze results of fact finding mission

Maintain situation map; brief Humanitarian Coordinator; post liaison officer if appropriate

Prepare for Initial Survey. Examine the feasibility of peace-keeping concept

Conduct preliminary analysis. Input in defining humanitarian assessment team, as appropriate.

Participate in humanitarian assessment as appropriate***

DPA

Analyze results of fact finding mission. Recommend political action as appropriate

Brief Humanitarian Coordinator

Analyze possibilities for preventive diplomacy/peacemaking initiative and design accordingly if appropriate

Recommend preventive diplomacy/peacemaking initiative to the SG

*** In circumstances where joint humanitarian/military assessment is necessary, particularly in the area of logistics

N.B. *While arrows indicate that interaction occurs between activities, the flow is not intended to convey absolute symmetry. Any Department may be in a different position in time or sequence, depending on the situation.*

93

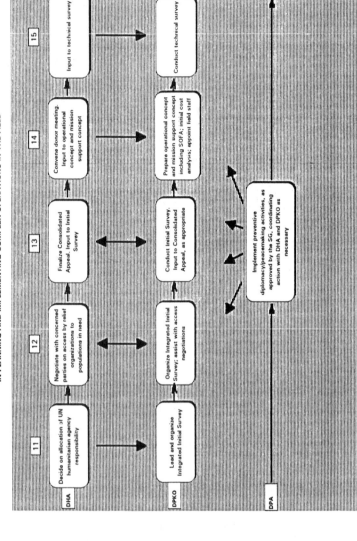

DRAFT

COORDINATION OF DHA, DPKO AND DPA ACTIVITIES
IN PLANNING AND IMPLEMENTING COMPLEX OPERATIONS IN THE FIELD

6 January 1995

DHA

| 11 | 12 | 13 | 14 | 15 |

11 — Decide on allocation of UN humanitarian agency responsibility

12 — Negotiate with concerned parties on access by relief organizations to populations in need

13 — Finalize Consolidated Appeal. Input to Initial Survey

14 — Convene donor meeting. Input to operational concept and mission support concept

15 — Input to technical survey

DPKO

Lead and organize Integrated Initial Survey

Organize Integrated Initial Survey; assist with access negotiations

Conduct Initial Survey. Input to Consolidated Appeal, as appropriate

Prepare operational concept and mission support concept including SOFA; initial cost analysis; appoint field staff

Conduct technical survey

DPA

Implement preventive diplomacy/peacemaking activities, as approved by the SG, coordinating action with DHA and DPKO as necessary

N.B. While arrows indicate that interaction occurs between activities, the flow is not intended to convey absolute symmetry. Any Department may be in a different position in time or sequence, depending on the situation.

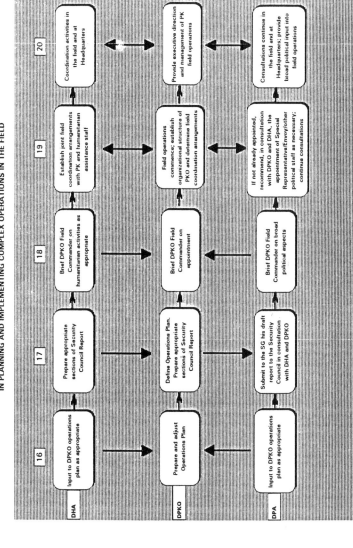

DRAFT

COORDINATION OF DHA, DPKO AND DPA ACTIVITIES
IN PLANNING AND IMPLEMENTING COMPLEX OPERATIONS IN THE FIELD

6 January 1995

16

DHA — Input to DPKO operations plan as appropriate

17 — Prepare appropriate sections of Security Council Report

18 — Brief DPKO Field Commander on humanitarian activities as appropriate

19 — Establish joint field coordination arrangements with PK and humanitarian assistance staff

20 — Coordination activities in the field and at Headquarters

DPKO — Prepare and adjust Operations Plan

Define Operations Plan. Prepare appropriate sections of Security Council Report

Brief DPKO Field Commander on appointment

Field operations commence; establish organizational structure of PKO and determine field coordination arrangements

Provide executive direction and management of PK field operations

DPA — Input to DPKO operations plan as appropriate

Submit to the SG his draft report to the Security Council in consultation with DHA and DPKO

Brief DPKO Field Commander on broad political aspects

If not already appointed, recommend, in consultation with DPKO and DHA, the appointment of Special Representative/Envoy/other political staff as necessary; continue consultations

Consultations continue in the field and at Headquarters; provide broad political input into field operations

N.B. While arrows indicate that interaction occurs between activities, the flow is not intended to convey absolute symmetry. Any Department may be in a different position in time or sequence, depending on the situation.

95

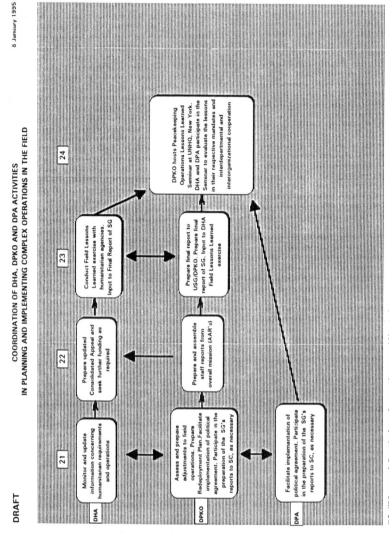

COORDINATION OF DHA, DPKO AND DPA ACTIVITIES
IN PLANNING AND IMPLEMENTING COMPLEX OPERATIONS IN THE FIELD

DRAFT

6 January 1995

21

DHA — Monitor and update information concerning humanitarian requirements and operations

22

Prepare updated Consolidated Appeal and seek further funding as required

23

Conduct Field Lessons Learned exercise with humanitarian agencies. Input to Final Report of SG

24

DPKO hosts Peacekeeping Operations Lessons Learned Seminar at UNHQ, New York. DHA and DPA participate in the Seminar to evaluate the lessons in their respective mandates and interdepartmental and interorganizational cooperation

DPKO — Assess and prepare adjustments to field operations. Prepare Redeployment Plan. Facilitate implementation of political agreement. Participate in the preparation of the SG's reports to SC, as necessary

Prepare and assemble staff reports from overall mission (AAR's)

Prepare final report to USG/DPKO. Prepare final report of SG. Input to DHA Field Lessons Learned exercise

DPA — Facilitate implementation of political agreement. Participate in the preparation of the SG's reports to SC, as necessary

N.B. While arrows indicate that interaction occurs between activities, the flow is not intended to convey absolute symmetry. Any Department may be in a different position in time or sequence, depending on the situation.

96

About the Author

Ambassador Edward Marks is a retired senior Foreign Service officer whose expertise is in management of autonomous organizations; cross-cultural and multilateral negotiation and interaction; and operating in and with international organizations. He is currently a Consulting Fellow at the Institute for National Strategic Studies and the Center for Strategic and International Studies and is affiliated with Cubic, Inc. Assignments in the Foreign Service included Deputy U.S. Representative, Economic and Social Council of the United Nations; Deputy Chief of Mission and Charge d'Affaires, U.S. Embassy to the Republics of Sri Lanka and the Maldives; and Ambassador, Republics of Guinea-Bissau and Cape Verde.

Ambassador Marks is the author of several articles on terrorism, the professional U.S. military officer, politics in South Asia, and multinational peacekeeping. He is also a frequent guest speaker for professional, business, and community organizations.